The Parent's Guide to SOCCER

DAN WOOG

**interior illustrations
by Jason Pederson**

ROXBURY PARK

LOWELL HOUSE
LOS ANGELES
NTC/Contemporary Publishing Group

Woog, Dan, 1953–
    The parent's guide to soccer / by Dan Woog.
      p.   cm.
    "A Roxbury Park book."
    Includes index.
    ISBN 0-7373-0047-7
    1. Soccer for children—United States. I. Title.
  GV944.2.W66   1999
  796.334'0973—dc21   98-50483
                   CIP

Published by Lowell House
A division of NTC/Contemporary Publishing Group, Inc.
4255 West Touhy Avenue, Lincolnwood (Chicago), Illinois 60646-1975 U.S.A.

Lowell House books can be purchased at special discounts when ordered in bulk for premiums and special sales. Contact Department CS at the following address:

NTC/Contemporary Publishing Group
4255 West Touhy Avenue
Lincolnwood, IL 60646-1975

Roxbury Park is a division of
NTC/Contemporary Publishing Group, Inc.

Managing Director and Publisher: Jack Artenstein
Editor in Chief, Roxbury Park Books: Michael Artenstein
Director of Publishing Services: Rena Copperman
Editorial Assistant: Nicole Monastirsky
Interior Illustrations: Jason Pederson
Typesetter: Carolyn Wendt

Printed and bound in the United States of America
10 9 8 7 6 5 4 3 2 1

CONTENTS

INTRODUCTION
Why Kids Love Soccer

The odds are good that you know your child pretty well. After all, you've lived with him or her for a few years; you've watched with varying degrees of pleasure, pain, and puzzlement as that son or daughter progressed from lying there to crawling, from toddling to running, from kicking cans and cats to reading, writing, and arithmetic.

And now it's back to running and kicking again. What's more, your son sleeps with his soccer ball; your daughter has posters of Kristine Lilly—a woman you'd never heard of but now know is one of the best soccer players in the world—hanging over her bed.

What's going on here?

What's going on is that the world's most popular game has come to America, and our children are leading the way. A number of trends have combined to make soccer this nation's fastest growing sport. You know it's happening—"soccer moms" are designated part of the electorate, every other commercial on TV features a minivan, a kid, and a soccer ball, and official statistics peg the number of youth soccer participants at over two million, putting it ahead of such "All-American" sports as basketball, football, and baseball—but you don't really understand why.

That's because you don't really understand soccer's appeal. And until you do, you won't understand why your child juggles in the living room, polishes his cleats each night in the middle of a room that looks like a war zone, and has heard of places—like Cameroon, Romania, and Trinidad and Tobago—that you yourself would have trouble finding on a map.

So why exactly is soccer such a great game for young boys and girls?

First, and above all else, it is fun to play. It requires almost constant running, something most young people love to do. Every player is involved in the game; there is no "right field" in soccer. Kicking a ball is a natural action; heading and controlling a ball are easily learned skills. And soccer knows no size limitations; a small, quick boy or girl can compete equally with a taller one.

The second reason children love soccer is it demands creativity and intelligence. In fact, when athletes are tested for these qualities, soccer players inevitably score higher than players of other sports. A soccer player must think for herself once the whistle blows. There are no set plays to run, no right or wrong paths to follow, no timeouts to interfere with the flow of the game. Each player is his own coach out on the field, and when the ultimate goal is reached—when eleven players meld themselves together, combining their individual efforts into crisp, clean team play—each person on the field feels he has contributed something physically, mentally, and emotionally to the mix.

Third, the equipment is relatively inexpensive, and modest in scope—in other words, nonthreatening to youngsters. It also lends itself easily to practice. Any child can juggle a soccer ball on her own, or devise impromptu games with neighborhood buddies; not everyone has a hockey rink or tennis court in the backyard.

Fourth, children sense that soccer players are part of an international family. Go anywhere in the world, produce a soccer ball, and you can find a friend. In addition, the nature of the sport and its adherents—friendly, adventuresome, cosmopolitan—lead to travel opportunities unavailable in most other sports.

Fifth, soccer can be played anyplace, in any season, by anyone. Tournaments are no longer limited to elite teams; in the words of the American Youth Soccer Organization, "Everybody plays." Another promising trend is rules modification for youngsters with physical and emotional disabilities.

Sixth, the rules are few, and easy to understand—except for offside, that is. (Don't worry; this book devotes plenty of space to that confusing restriction!)

Seventh, soccer is a tough, physically demanding sport, but it is not violent. A player feels exhausted after a match and is often bruised—but she still lines up readily to shake her opponent's hand, exchange patches or jerseys, and talk and laugh about the game.

These are some of the reasons your child is passionate about soccer. Once you understand the sport's appeal you can begin to share that passion. You do not need to have grown up with soccer to experience its power. All you need is an open mind, a sense of excitement, a love of competition and adventure, and style and grace. And, oh yes—this book should help too!

CHAPTER 1
First Things First

If you're already involved in youth soccer—that is, if you've simultaneously winced and laughed at your first view of swarmball, that horde of tots chasing a ball nearly as big as themselves; if you've sliced your first orange, driven to your first field in a part of the state you never knew existed, or had to supply your first birth certificate for a laborious, time-consuming, nit-picking registration process—you can skip this chapter.

BEFORE YOUR CHILD BEGINS SOCCER

If, however, you're still contemplating whether to sign young Caitlin or Charles up for the local youth soccer program, read on. You might even want to commit what you read to memory. On second thought, you should.

Keep in Mind

Before registering your child in a youth soccer program, be sure to consider the following advice.

There Is No "Right Age" to Begin One child may begin playing soccer at six, another may wait until ten or twelve. Beginning early is no guarantee of future success or enjoyment, let alone college scholarship offers. Each child is different. Key factors include the child's maturity level (both physical and emotional) and the maturity levels of the adults running the program.

Be Clear About the Objective of the Program The primary objective of a youth soccer program should be teaching skills—not winning. A healthy, happy learning environment will do more to hook a child on soccer (and keep him hooked) than a "championship season" his first time out.

It should go without saying—but, unfortunately, it must be said—that a child's first soccer experience should not involve traveling enormous distances, publishing scores and standings in newspapers, awarding trophies only to the top team, and cheerleaders yelling their lungs out. That level of competitiveness comes later.

Fortunately, more and more youth soccer organizations are scaling down their introductory programs. Many youth leagues do not even keep score, or else they reorganize teams so often that comparative scores become meaningless. Across North America, the watchword is fun, not win.

Make sure the program you are enrolling your child in has a philosophy you are comfortable with. Then consider these points:

A Beginning Program Should Not Demand an Enormous Time Commitment There are two reasons for this. First, your child undoubtedly has other activities and needs time to pursue them with a minimal amount of pressure. Just as important, however, is every youngster's need to daydream and to play spontaneously with friends, unbound by adult supervision and interference.

Enrolling a Child in an Organized Activity Does Mean a Certain Obligation of Time Before signing any papers, be aware how many hours, days, weeks, and months the program will involve, when and how far from your home practices and games will be held, and what time conflicts may need to be resolved in order to get your child to as many of them as humanly possible.

Think Ahead How You Will React If Things Don't Go As You Had Hoped Ask yourself a few difficult questions: How will you feel if your child is less than stellar? What if the coach is overbearing or uncommunicative? What if your son or daughter wants to quit? Such situations often arise. Thinking about them beforehand, and preparing for their very real possibility, saves plenty of anguish down the road.

Think Through What It Means to Be a Fan at a Game What kinds of comments are you apt to make on the sidelines: "That's all right, Jackson, keep your head up"? Or "C'mon, Jackson, can't you keep your eyes on the ball? What's the matter with you today?" Don't laugh. Some parents simply cannot stop themselves from making inappropriate comments. If you don't feel you can be a supportive parent, consider staying home.

Ask Yourself If You Are Willing to Become an Informed Spectator Some parents have grown up with soccer; others don't know the difference between the center circle and the Arctic Circle. You can help your child immeasurably by educating yourself. (You'll also help yourself by getting a great deal more out of those many soccer mornings, afternoons, and evenings.) If you're not willing to make a minimal commitment to learn about the game, you can't help but negatively affect your child's overall soccer experience.

Find Out How Much You Will Be Expected to Participate Some youth programs make parental participation mandatory, whether in the form of lining the field, working the food stand, or refereeing. Some youth programs "strongly encourage" parental volunteers. Even if your program does not require you to participate formally, you'll still be called upon to carpool, make phone calls, and perform innumerable other tasks. Make sure you have time to shoulder your share of the burden.

Be Ready to Serve As a Role Model, Even If You Never Set Foot on the Field Coaches are not the only ones who teach the importance of teamwork and commitment; parents do too. The firmness and consistency with which mothers and fathers model fair play, good sportsmanship, goal setting, and respect go a long way toward determining to what extent their children enjoy soccer and, in a way, all sports. It's not an easy task—but whoever said youth soccer was all fun and games?

Recognize that there are lots of reasons for children to play soccer, many of which have nothing to do with scoring goals and winning games. Youth soccer—and most other sports, of course—teach many things, including

➤ Learning to compete within a set of rules.
➤ Learning what it means—and takes—to become physically fit.
➤ Learning to release energy in a constructive way.
➤ Learning to handle winning and losing.
➤ Learning to understand the feelings and attitudes of others.
➤ Learning self-control and self-discipline.
➤ Learning to set a goal, and then reach it.

> ➤ Learning to handle pressure.
> ➤ Learning commitment and loyalty.

How to Introduce Your Child to Soccer

So you've considered commitments and consequences, and you still want soccer in your child's—and your—life. Here are a few hints for how to introduce the game:

It's Never Too Early to Start Teaching a Child to Move Around In this era of designer cribs and strollers, we tend to confine youngsters to specific spaces just at the age they're beginning to move around independently. Encourage infants to use their bodies as much as possible; when they're ready to begin kicking and running, this will come in handy.

Playing Is the Best Physical Education of All Tag, kicking a Nerf ball, tug-of-war with string—all of these teach movement and coordination. Within the bounds of safety, provide little children opportunities to walk, run, climb, lift, throw, and kick. As children get older, programs that teach movement skills in a nonstructured way are recommended. These abound at YMCAs, day care centers, and the like. What's especially fortunate (from a soccer point of view) is that infants, toddlers, and little children naturally have good eye-foot coordination; it's the eye-hand coordination that is difficult for most. Meanwhile, it's easy for tots to kick a ball and run after it—and it's fun for them too. So make sure that toddlers get little balls to play with. Encourage them to kick the balls, and then enjoy the results.

Avoid Structured Lessons or Sport Leagues While they endorse "movement" classes, most experts on childhood frown on structured lessons

Footnotes

How young can children start playing? The youngest appropriate age seems to be four. That's what one Maryland youth organization decided—though not without controversy. They devised a progression program starting with four- and five-year-olds, three to a "team." (The teams are actually called "soccer play groups.") At every session the children play "scrimmage games," with players constantly changing sides and no scores being kept. Players learn to become "friends" with the ball on a 20 x 30 field. At the same time, parents are taught a variety of games they can play at home with their youngsters. One of the most popular is tag (with and without soccer balls), because it teaches balance.

First and second graders also play 3 v. 3, but on a slightly larger (30 x 30) field. One unique feature is goalposts on all four sides, which means there is plenty of scoring.

Third and fourth graders play either 4 v. 4 or 5 v. 5, depending on available numbers, on a 40 x 40 field, while fifth and sixth graders play anywhere from 5 v. 5 to 7 v. 7 on a 70 x 50 field.

Parents are solicited as volunteer coaches. Several "coaching clinics" are offered each year. In addition, a motor development specialist helps parent/coaches assess when players are ready for new challenges.

or sports leagues for children younger than six or seven. The reasons are legion, and include frustration (especially in children whose motor ability is not as advanced as others), boredom (either now, if the child is not emotionally ready, or later, after he or she has played on a dozen or so teams before high school), pressure (young children are not equipped to handle the demands of performance that leagues often induce), and physical injury (in a structured setting it's difficult for little children to ask to stop playing because of fatigue or pain).

Perhaps the most important reason not to begin structured soccer play before six or seven is that children any younger are simply not emotionally ready. They do not fully grasp the concepts of competition, winning and losing, playing, and sitting out that are inevitable parts of instruction and participation in leagues. They'd rather be running around on their own, playing games of their own invention and then moving on to something else when the spirit moves them, than be confined to a rigorous "program," no matter how well-intentioned and ably organized.

Formal Training

When *should* a child receive "formal training" in organized sports?

When the Motivation to Play Comes from the Child, Not the Parent
This does not mean the child must initiate the idea of signing up or participating. However, he or she should be the one to decide whether it is enjoyable and worth continuing when the program is offered again.

When Parents Are Ready Formal training can begin when parents are ready to help their children participate in a program that is appropriate to the child's—not the parent's—age, ability, and physical and psychological development. Parents should resist the urge to "create a champion." Talent emerges naturally; players have plenty of time to develop skills in later years. They do not have to start before they (or their parents) are ready.

THE BASICS

Do you feel like a soccer dunce? Are you confused about some of the basics of soccer but embarrassed to ask? Don't be! If you haven't grown up with the game, how would you know how it's played?

Learn the Fundamentals

It's a Ball-and-Goal Game The object is to get the ball in the other team's goal—using any part of the body except the hands—and to keep it out of your own.

There Are Eleven Players on the Field at Any One Time They include forwards (also called strikers), midfielders, defenders (or full-backs), and a goalkeeper (or goalie or keeper). There are no set numbers of players for each position—except goalkeeper, there being only one. The *keeper* is the only player allowed to use his or her hands—and then only in a certain area, called the penalty box.

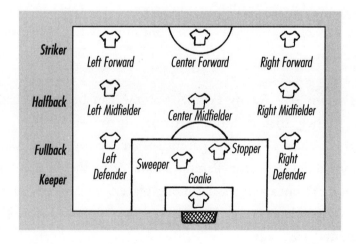

Some Soccer Is Played with Fewer than Eleven Players This is called *small-sided* or *short-sided* soccer. It generally involves teams of four, five, or six players (called "4 v. 4," "5 on 5," etc.). Small-sided soccer is used both for training purposes—players in short-sided games get many more *touches* on the ball and thus improve rapidly—and for lessening the competitive pressures of a full-sized game. However, the techniques and tactics used in small-sided soccer are the same as those used in 11 v. 11 soccer. All soccer is essentially a duel between small groups of players.

There Is No Standard Size for a Soccer Field International regulations call for a field to be between 100 and 130 yards long and 50 to 100 yards wide. That is an enormous variation, and a game played on a long, wide field is apt to be quite different from one played on a short, narrow one. But that's all part of soccer's appeal: Each game is unique. (Short-goal games, mentioned above, are naturally played in smaller areas.)

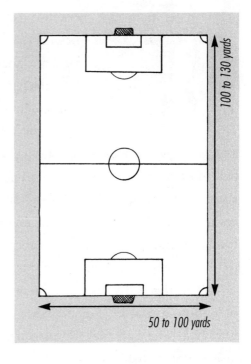

100 to 130 yards

50 to 100 yards

There Is, However, a Standard-size Goal Goals are eight feet high and eight yards wide. (When goals are used in small-sided games—and they do not have to be—they are smaller.) The area in front of the goal, where a goalkeeper can use her hands, is forty-four yards wide

and extends eighteen yards from the goal line. The smaller box inside the large penalty area is used only to determine the spot from where a goal kick (see below) is taken.

All Lines Are "in Play" In other words, a ball must cross completely over a sideline or end line to be called out of bounds, and a ball must cross completely over the goal line in order to count as a goal. If the referee is unsure whether or not the whole ball passed over the whole line, he should not award a goal.

When the ball goes out of bounds over the sideline, the opposing team takes a *throw-in*. There are several requirements for a legal throw—for example, the feet must remain on the ground, the ball must be thrown from behind the head in one fluid motion, and there can be no spin to the ball—which are all difficult for young players to do. If the throw-in team makes an illegal throw, the throw-in reverts to the other team. A team cannot score directly off a throw-in (to do so would take an enormous throw, anyway).

When the ball goes out of bounds over the end line as the result of a shot or pass by the attacking team, the defending team takes a *goal kick*. The ball may be placed anywhere in the small *goal area* inside the penalty box, and a player—usually the keeper or a defender—plays the ball out, either long or to a nearby defender.

When the ball is kicked out of bounds over the end line by the defending team (usually this is a mistake, although sometimes a defender knocks it out just to escape from danger), the attacking team takes a *corner kick*. The ball is placed anywhere in the small arc on the corner of the field and is struck toward the goal.

There Are Two Different Types of Fouls in Soccer Both are penalized by *free kicks*. Direct kicks are awarded for fouls that involve physical contact—for example, tripping, kicking, or shoving an opponent. Direct kicks are also awarded for hand balls (touching the ball with the hand, arm, or shoulder). For direct kicks, the team fouled takes a free kick—they hit a stationary ball—and can score directly off that kick, without anyone else touching it.

When a direct-kick foul occurs in the large penalty area, and the foul was committed by the attacking team, the result is a *penalty kick*. The ball is placed twelve yards from the goal, and one player is allowed a free shot on goal. The keeper cannot move forward until the ball is kicked. Though penalty kicks look easy, the pressure on the shooter is enormous, and the best players in the world have been known to miss.

Indirect kicks, the other type of foul, do not involve physical contact. Examples of indirect kicks include dangerous play (putting oneself or an opponent in danger, without contact), obstruction (not allowing an opponent to play the ball), unsportsmanlike conduct, and foul language. For indirect kicks, the team fouled against takes a free kick, but in order for a goal to count, at least one other player (on either team) must also touch the ball. An indirect-kick foul that occurs in the large penalty area is treated like any other indirect kick; there is no special provision for taking this kick.

For all free kicks, direct or indirect, the defending team must line up at least ten yards away from the ball (or on the goal line, if the indirect kick is taken less than ten yards from the goal). Defenders often form a *wall*, standing shoulder to shoulder to create as much of an obstacle as they can for the shooter.

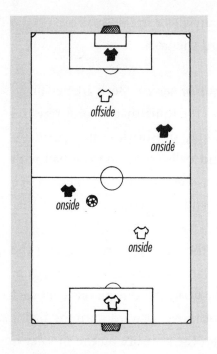

***One of the Most Complicated Calls in Soccer Is* Offside** The purpose of offside is to prevent goal hanging. Basically, a player is offside if there aren't at least two defenders (usually one of them is the goalkeeper) between her and the goal, *and* the ball is on her half of the field, *and* she is part of the play (in other words, if a player is in an offside position but lies injured on the side of the field, and none of the defenders attempts to mark her, then offside should not be called). Offside is called only on a shot or a pass, not on a dribble, which theoretically gives a player in an offside position time enough to scramble back *onside*.

Offside is a complex rule, and its interpretation is never easy. Our advice: Don't obsess about offside. It causes spectators more problems than it solves.

Referees Are in Complete Charge of the Game They even keep time; there is no official scoreboard clock in soccer. (Regulation halves are forty-five minutes long; younger players play shorter games.) Referees also have the discretion of invoking the advantage rule: If, in the referee's mind, a team that was fouled against would lose an attacking advantage if he called a foul, he can yell, "Play on!" That acknowledges he saw the foul but wants play to continue so that the attacking team can continue to go toward the goal.

Referees' authority extends to warning and ejecting players. A *yellow card* is shown as a stern warning. It is given, for example, for an unduly strong tackle or after repeated fouls. In many leagues, two yellow cards in one game result in ejection from the match.

A *red card* is the ultimate punishment: A player receiving a red card is immediately banished from a game. Red cards are shown for exceptionally flagrant fouls, fighting, and other unseemly conduct. In some leagues, players who receive red cards must appear before a disciplinary board before they can play again.

POSITIONS

First off, all players, no matter what their position, should have the technical ability to receive a ball and play it under pressure in a limited space. A boy or girl who can control a ball with any part of the body and immediately prepare for the next step—whether a dribble, pass, or shot—is a true soccer player. And that is true anywhere on the field.

Strikers

Strikers (also called forwards, front-runners, or attackers) are the soccer players who score the most. They tend to get their names in the paper more than others. Theirs are the names everyone knows.

Though putting the ball in the net is important, the best forwards also perform other functions. They are the first line of defense—if they can pin their opponents deep in the foes' end, then win the ball, they've saved their teammates sixty to eighty yards of work. They must learn to pass as well as shoot—and know when to do one or the other. At times, strikers *should* take defenders on by dribbling; at other times, their best choice is to lay the ball off to a more open teammate. It is not easy to be both selfish ("Shoot!") and selfless ("Pass!").

Nor is it as easy as it looks to score—even on an open net (try it yourself some time; then add the pressure of a game). Strikers have to be able to seize scoring opportunities (and half chances) in the split second these become available. Their shots must be struck with accuracy and power. They should also be able to cross from the wings, which means they must understand the complex principles of width, depth, mobility, and penetration. Strikers need to be levelheaded, quick thinking, quick playing (though not necessarily blindingly fast), agile, patient (because they almost always fail to score), and able to handle pressure at least as well as goalkeepers do.

The Goalkeeper

The Goalkeeper is the most vulnerable player on a team. He or she is the one everyone sees freeze as a striker zooms in unmolested on a breakaway, then trudges to fetch the ball from the back of the net after a goal is scored. No one remembers the missed tackle at midfield that lead to the breakaway; all eyes (and tongues) focus on the keeper who "let the goal in." And even if a keeper has a magnificent game—save all but one or two shots—when it is all over, most fans remember the goals, not the saves.

That is a tough break for parents on the sidelines—and tougher still for the player. But some youngsters love playing goal. They enjoy the pressure of an onrushing breakaway. They love to dive in the mud to tip a shot wide and leap high to shovel a ball over the top of the goal. They have good eye-hand coordination, to go along with the fine foot skills that keepers need. (Long gone are the days when goalies *picked up* or guarded against passes from their teammates; today they must be as adept with their feet as with their hands.) They enjoy telling their defenders who to pick up and where to move, they get a thrill out of being in command of the goalie box, and they are excited—not overwhelmed—when they face down a penalty kicker just twelve yards away.

Playing goalkeeper is not for everyone. Certain personality types cannot handle pressure well. Others do not like feeling apart from field players, or they simply lack the physical attributes (decent size, good hands, quick reflexes, upper body strength) required of keepers.

Because goalkeeper is a pressure-filled position, and because it can be so frustrating—especially for a smaller player faced with the task of defending an enormous area—most youth soccer experts advise *not* specializing in goal before the age of twelve or so. By rotating every player on a team in and out of goal, the thinking goes, one or two players will not be singled out for pressure or blame. At the same time, all players will be exposed to the demands of the position, and all will be taught the foot skills required of all soccer players.

Defenders

In addition to shutting down the opposition's attack, defenders initiate their own team's offense. The job of a defender is not to simply boot the ball long; it is to win the ball, possess it, then begin moving it upfield intelligently and with poise.

Good defenders must be disciplined enough to understand marking assignments (which opponents they must guard)—plus the important principles of delay, depth (how close you play the opponent), concentration, balance, control, and restraint—yet be flexible enough to see a dangerous situation developing, intelligent enough to solve it on their own, and confident enough to be quick about it. They must know instinctively when to play tight man-to-man marking (this male-oriented term is used even by girls) and when to move into a zone. They must remain focused on one or two opponents at all times, yet keep the entire field in view. (That is why hearing-impaired youngsters often gravitate to defense: Most of the action is in front of them, so they need not rely on verbal communication as much as midfielders or strikers.)

Defenders must quickly shake off being bested; instead of hanging their head when an opponent beats them, they must race back into play and try to minimize the damage. Defenders must be unselfish, because most of the time they don't receive any praise or even much notice. They must be physically strong as well as willing to step in front of an attacker and make a tackle. They must be confident in the air, since defenders *head* more than other players. And they must be fast. These days, coaches often place their fleetest—not their slowest—athletes on defense.

Midfielders

Midfielders have more contact with the ball more often than other players. They also do more running than anyone else on the field. They are the links between defenders and forwards; though all soccer players are expected to play both offense and defense, midfielders do so more equally than others. They are also responsible for maintaining as well as changing the pace of the game (fast, slow, or in-between) and for orchestrating a challenging mix of short passes and long crosses.

Midfielders must possess vision (ability to see what is happening all around), the ability to switch play when necessary, and an understanding not only of the transition game (switching from offense to defense and back again), but of their role in it. In addition to intelligence and a keen game sense, they must have excellent techniques, such as the ability to pass with accuracy, and know when to take opponents on—and when not to.

ENCOURAGING YOUR CHILD TO SET GOALS

Goals clearly marked on the field provide a physical target for soccer players. Just as important, however, are individual or team goals that youngsters should aim for. Though they won't always reach those goals, part of the joy of soccer lies in the shots we take.

Here's how to help youngsters set up goals that are bigger—and far more rewarding—than the 8 x 24 ones we usually talk about.

Setting Goals

Avoid Scoring- or Honors-Oriented Goals Encourage your child to set goals. It's easy for a child to become disappointed if she does not score a dozen times in a season or fails to win the Most Valuable Player award. However, if her goal is to improve her weak footwork, earn more playing time, or learn a new position, that is achievable—not to mention more realistic and valuable.

Goals Can Be Both Short-Term and Long-Term Short-term goals can usually be accomplished without much trouble: adding a half mile to a player's daily workout routine, taking ten penalty kicks after each practice, learning how to make a legal throw-in. Long-term goals require more attention and persistence: running a certain number of stop-and-gos in a particular time, becoming the number one penalty kicker on the team, throwing the ball farther than anyone else.

Goals Can Be Both Technical and Personal Technical goals include better heading, passing, shooting, running, and jumping. Examples of personal goals are coming prepared to play, being more attentive to the coach, and getting along better with teammates.

Don't Forget Team Goals These can include winning against a team your child's team has yet to beat, or qualifying for the league playoffs. Setting team goals can help unify a group of youngsters and keep them unified when the going gets tough. Try encouraging your child to help his team set group goals.

Make Sure the Goals Are Your Child's, Not Yours Parents often assume that what they want out of soccer is the same thing their child wants. But that is not always the case. A parent may want the team to win every game and then the league championship; a player may care more about improving her skills so that she can make the high school varsity the following season. Children are more motivated to reach a goal, and to be satisfied with their success, when it's a goal they care about. That's why it is so important to let a youngster set her own goals.

Don't Nag Goals are private things. Let your child keep his goals to himself. He'll share his accomplishments with you if you give him room to achieve them on his own. If you continually hound him— "You're making progress on those goals, aren't you, Jimmy boy?"— he will resent both you and the goals he is supposed to want to achieve.

Affirm the Value of Having Goals Plant the idea of goals in your child's mind and cite a few examples—but don't overdo it. Adults tend to assume that either children know everything (how to set goals, for example) or they know nothing (they have no clue how to figure out their own goals). Give your child a start, then trust her to come up with her own aspirations. After all, soccer is your child's game—not yours.

COMMON MISCONCEPTIONS

No parent would ever dream of telling a young baseball player, "Just close your eyes when you swing, honey, and pray you hit the ball." Nor would any parent offer this advice: "Just smack that golf ball as hard as you can. Chances are it'll go wherever you want it to."

Yet plenty of well-meaning parents give less-than-sound, and even counterproductive, advice on soccer. Of course, that's natural; most moms and dads have not grown up with the game.

Some Common Misconceptions

"Just Boot It out of There!" In fact, banging the ball blindly upfield is rarely a good idea. Only in the most dire of circumstances will coaches want their players to blast the ball away. Most want their young charges to learn how to pass the ball out of the backfield, away from danger yet still in control.

This achieves two aims. First, it helps players develop ball skills and poise under pressure. Second, it increases the chances of retaining possession. When teammates or fans yell, "Kill it! Give it a ride!" they might as well be saying, "Give it to the other team!" That's because the opponents are most likely facing the play, ready to receive the ball, while the kicker's teammates are running away, their backs to the action.

So a better piece of advice is "Pass it out of there!"

This advice also applies to goalkeepers. Many coaches like their keepers to pass the ball effectively, either by rolling it to a nearby defender or utilizing a baseball-type throw to an open player. Neither method is as flashy as a long boom-kick, nor does it achieve the same distance, but it is much safer.

"Just Go Straight up the Middle!" This common shout aggravates many coaches. Attacking down the middle is one of the most difficult plays in all of soccer. Usually the center of the field is where a team's strongest players converge; it's almost always where players mount their toughest defense. Coaches like to attack up the flanks when possible, to take advantage of open space. Just because the middle is the most direct route does not always make it the best.

That said, however, don't clamor for the ball to be played into the far corner every time. When a team relies on that attack strategy alone, it becomes very predictable. If Cindi goes into the corner a few times, great; the next time she gets the ball, pray silently (don't shout) that she'll confound her opponent by cutting sharply into the middle (either by dribbling the ball there herself, or making a pass there). In other words, the more a team makes use of a wide variety of options, the more they'll fluster the opposing side.

Finally, here is one more way in which soccer is not like American football. Can you imagine the San Francisco 49ers ever deliberately playing the ball backward? In soccer, however, knocking the ball backward to an open player is often a great play. It is in fact a superb way to set up an attack.

"Sticking to Your Position on the Field Is Crucial" Not always. Soccer is not like football, where a highly specialized player (say, a nose tackle) has a highly defined role. Nor is it like baseball, where a first baseman must always position himself in a certain spot to field a ball or receive a throw. Soccer is not even like the relatively free-flowing sport of basketball, where a guard is almost always expected to trail the play upcourt.

True, a soccer match would degenerate if all eleven players freelanced merrily about the field. But part of the appeal of the sport is that it allows for more creativity, innovation, and on-field improvisation than any of the games mentioned above. If your son or daughter—young Dylan or Deirdre Defender—races upfield past midfielders, don't panic; relax and enjoy the show. Chances are he or she has been coached to do exactly that and has already made sure a teammate is covering on defense in back.

Similarly, get out of the habit of thinking of your young striker as a *left wing, center forward,* or *right wing.* In the modern game, lateral movement up front is not only encouraged, it's demanded. Your children are learning sophisticated strategies—and no doubt enjoying the heck out of it.

"Offside Is an Automatic Call" No way. Offside is as much a judgment call as anything else in soccer. Not only must two defenders be between the ball and the goal, but also the person in the offside position must be gaining an advantage by being where he is. In other words, the defenders must be aware of him *and* must be affected by his position. If a player is offside but not calling for the ball (or expecting to receive it), and a defender does not move to cover him, chances are the officials won't call him on it—howls of protest by parents to the contrary.

Similarly, an official will not declare the offside infraction until the ball is played; in other words, offside will not be called while a player is still dribbling. (When the ball is played means when a pass is made or a shot taken.) So save your yelps at the official until the player with the ball gives it off—and then check to make certain the apparent offender was truly involved in the play.

Referees Call Too Much, or They Call Too Little These are probably the two most common spectator complaints. In fact, calling a youth soccer match demands considerable judgment. Among the factors a referee must weigh when deciding whether or not to call a foul are the age and gender of the players, their relative level of skill, the intensity of the contest, the context of the infraction, and whether an advantage was gained either by the fouling team or the team fouled against.

A foul in a coed recreational game is not the same as a foul in the World Cup. An isolated infraction that might simply have been a slip-up early in the match is not the same as a premeditated retaliatory foul late in a close game. A slight push after which the player retains possession is not the same as a vicious sliding tackle from behind. And retaining possession is different when in front of the goal a player is aiming for than in front of one he is defending with his life.

One other note about refereeing: The man in the middle is the official timekeeper, true—but unlike other sports, he has the authority to keep the game going because of delays, both unintentional (injury, dog on the field, ball in the poison ivy) and intentional by the team in the lead (the old "I'll take the throw-in," "No, you take it" trick). In soccer, time limits are merely guidelines, not strict boundaries. So shrieking, "Hey ref, wasn't that half a little long?" is not only impolite, it's misguided.

"A Child Should Choose One Position Early, and then Stick to It"

Most experts agree such a philosophy is harmful to a child's development as a player. A coach who shifts players around actually aids everyone's development in the game, by exposing them to its many disparate elements. Soccer players are expected to both attack and defend and, when called upon, to be able to do either anywhere in the field.

This argument against specialization is especially true when applied to young goalkeepers. Some of the world's top coaches believe that the pressure of the position is so great that no one should specialize in it until he or she reaches thirteen or fourteen—an age when the decision to play goal is truly the player's, not the coach's or parents'. And in today's game, when what goalkeepers do with their feet is nearly as important as what they do with their hands, it is important for players to acquire those skills at an early age. And the best way to do that is by playing in the field.

"My Kid Is So Great at Twelve, He's Sure to Get a College Scholarship"

This statement is fraught with danger. For one thing, success at the U-12, or under-twelve (years old), level has little to do with what happens six years down the line. A young player may burn out because of too much competition or because of too much scrutiny at such an early age. He might discover something that interests him more than soccer—lacrosse, the piano, skateboards, medicine—and either stop playing completely or scale back his commitment. Or—horrors!—he may be the best player on his particular team or in his local league but not that spectacular in wider competition.

Another misconception involves the idea of scholarships. Colleges are severely limited in the number of "rides" they are allowed to offer; even those schools that can offer the maximum (which is far fewer than for football and other sports) usually do not fund all suitable applicants—or else they spread out the funds so that no one player receives the full amount.

Furthermore, anyone who participates in youth soccer in order to win a college scholarship is motivated wrongly. There are many reasons for youngsters to play soccer—physical exertion, camaraderie, the joy of kicking, to name just a few—but paying for a college education should not be one of them. Parents who direct their children this way place an unfair burden on them, and at the same time set themselves up for disappointment.

"When You're Hurt, Put Heat on Your Injury" No, no, a trillion times no! Heat (hot towels, heating pads, warm baths, etc.) can aggravate most injuries. Heat draws blood to an injured area, lengthening the amount of time it takes swelling to go down and raising the chances an injury will turn into a hematoma (blood-filled swelling under the skin) that can last for weeks. So forget heat—at least for the first forty-eight hours following an injury.

Instead, for minor injuries apply ice (in the form of an ice pack or frozen into paper cups) to the affected area for forty-eight hours; for moderate to severe sprains, strains, and contusions, apply ice for seventy-two to ninety-six hours. Ice should be applied for fifteen to twenty minute periods, with an equal amount of time between applications. Not until several days have passed and swelling has been reduced should heat be applied; only then will it aid in the healing process.

"When You're Exercising in Hot Weather, Take Plenty of Salt Tablets" This belief is a holdover from the days when football was played without pads. Today we know that salt tablets, because of their high salt concentration, actually draw fluids out of the circulatory system and dehydrate the body. The result? Possibly stomach cramps.

The key to replacing fluids lost by sweat is to drink plenty of fluids. Soccer players—all athletes, in fact—should take short but frequent water breaks, because the intestines can absorb only a certain amount of fluid at a time. Thirst should not be used as an indicator for water intake; a body needs water long before such signals reach the brain. So players should be encouraged to drink even when they aren't thirsty— about eight glasses of fluids (preferably water) the day before as well as the day of a game. More should be consumed on hot, humid days.

"Soccer Is Not a Contact Sport" Dead wrong—there is plenty of contact in soccer. Whether it's little kids bumping into each other, eleven-year-olds misdirecting the ball into teammates' shins, teenagers knocking into each other during particularly forceful tackles and while contesting head balls, or World Cup professionals aggressively swiping at opponents' ankles, knees, groins, and other body parts, soccer is indeed a physical game. The best take on the topic goes something like this: "Football is a violent sport. Soccer is a contact sport. Bridge is a noncontact sport."

F o o t n o t e s

The times they are a-changin': Nine out of ten Americans say they would be proud if their daughter became a professional athlete—the exact same percentage as for sons.

CHAPTER 2
Knowing Your Child

This may shock some parents, but there is always more than one child on the field during a soccer match. Sometimes the game is played with four or five on a team; sometimes with eleven. But there is never just one.

ASSESSING YOUR CHILD'S ABILITY

It is often hard for sideline-pacing moms and dads to notice the other players out there—and harder still for them to judge how their child measures up. Objectivity has never been a hallmark of parenthood, and youth soccer is no exception.

No one is asking parents to marshal statistics to rate their child against her teammates. They (statistics, that is) often lie. Besides, soccer—with its low scoring and free-flowing nature—is not a game of figures. The number of goals a flashy forward scores is no more important than the number of goals a quiet, well-positioned defender prevents—though you can measure the former and not the latter. It is impossible to tally how many times a player makes a good decision as

Footnotes

One of the age-old youth soccer questions involves the issue of "playing up": In other words, should Ashley step up from the U-12 age division to U-14?

It's a tough call, especially when parents and coaches disagree. Some mothers and fathers might want a child to play up in order to gain greater experience, tougher competition, and (for parents as well as players) ego satisfaction. Other parents prefer their child to stay in her own age group so she can play with friends or (perhaps) continue as the star she has been for so long.

Coaches may want a child to play up in order to help their team or out of a genuine interest in seeing that youngster improve. Or they might advise against playing up in order to help their team or out of a genuine interest in the child being coached with the younger age group.

Some coaches solve the "playing up" problem by moving an entire team into a higher age group. They must then explain to parents what the team will lose in the short term (games) will be more than compensated for by what the players will gain in the long term (experience, skills, life lessons).

One team choosing that route was Sparta in northern Illinois. They spent their formative U-16 and U-17 years playing up at U-19 in prestigious tournaments, taking their lumps yet learning along the way. Their decision paid off. They ended up winning a national championship. A couple of weeks later they were invited to represent the United States at a tournament in China—a women's tournament played in 50,000-seat stadiums. They held their own and had a wonderful three-week experience. None of that would have happened had they not risked playing up.

opposed to a bad one or how often one teammate provides defensive cover for another.

Which is not to say that parents don't try. The father of the striker who leads the team in goals has bragging rights at his weekly golf game; the dad whose daughter consistently delivers the pass that leads to the pass that leads to the goal too often remains silent. The mother of the goalkeeper knows exactly how many shutouts her son has turned in during the season; the mom of the defender who keeps clearing balls off the line rarely keeps tabs.

How then can you determine where your child stands relative to his or her teammates?

A better question is, Why should you? Youth soccer should not be a competition to determine the "best" player on a team; it should be about improvement—each player individually, and the team as a whole—and having fun. Parents should avoid getting caught up in a rating game, where each player competes against every other player on the field. Parents should instead try to assess their child's ability based on the following very subjective measures—and they should keep in mind that every youngster develops physically, mentally, and emotionally at his or her own pace.

Skill

Does he use both feet when he kicks or rely only on one? Does she use the inside of her foot for short passes, the instep (laces) to drive the ball? Does he feel comfortable controlling a high ball with any part of his body? Does she head well, or does she flinch and shy away (or simply choose not to head at all)? Is he a confident dribbler, or does he always pass off the instant he gets the ball? Does she place her shots consistently on goal (if not necessarily hitting it), or do most of her shots fly high or wide?

Running Ability

There are various different kinds of speed, such as short distance (racing away from a defender or sprinting back to catch an attacker), long distance (going from one end of the field to the other), and acceleration (the first two steps being the most important). Another factor in running ability is stamina. Some children run all day, while others tire easily. One more point: A child who runs the entire game often runs needlessly. Running for the sake of motion is not the mark of a polished soccer player.

Game Sense

A complete soccer player works both offense and defense, no matter where on the field she is. In other words, a good striker must also be able to pen an opposing fullback into the defensive end. Similarly, a good defender must be adept at initiating an attack, carrying the ball himself or outletting it (passing off) to an open player. A complete soccer player will call for the ball and make good runs to get it, but she will also urge a teammate to pass to someone else and make dummy runs (clearing a defender out of the way with no expectation of receiving a pass herself). A complete soccer player will position himself intelligently on the field though this is difficult to notice, because a well-placed player does not need to run a lot. And a complete player may not always make the right play—but when she makes a mistake, she keeps her head up and tries her hardest to compensate for it.

Happiness

Perhaps the most important quality to watch for in a player is joy. If your child plays soccer with a smile on his face, it does not matter one bit whether he is a starter or a reserve, the star or the scrub. All that counts is that he is measuring himself against his own standards and finds he is doing fine.

WHEN YOUR CHILD IS A SUPERSTAR

So your son or daughter is a superstar. Congratulations—but calm down. It's wonderful that young Donovan or Delia is the best player on the team, however, it is not the most spectacular thing in the world. Your progeny has not discovered a cure for cancer or AIDS; besides, he or she is still just a child. Success at the youth level does not necessarily translate into a World Cup starting berth, or success at every other endeavor. You should be able to enjoy your youngster's achievements, yet at the same time stay objective about the experience.

Tips for the Superstar Player

Your Child's Success Is Not Your Own While you have indeed raised a superb young soccer player, you are not the person out on the field scoring goals, setting them up, or preventing them. You are not the one who practices long and hard honing skills or runs several miles a day to get in tip-top shape. Those are *her* accomplishments; much as you have encouraged her, you must resist feeling over-invested in her success. Just as important as not obsessing over the downsides of their child's experience with the game, parents ought not boost their own egos based on their child's skill in the sport.

Situations Change The boy who stands astride the soccer world today may be supplanted by someone else tomorrow. That is not to say he will suddenly turn into a poor player; it simply means that early success in soccer (or anything else) is no predictor of what will happen several months or years later. Children develop at different rates physically, mentally, and emotionally. Interests and enthusiasms wax and wane. Coaches come and go; teams fade and flourish. Families move. Injuries happen. Even changes in the rules can have an effect:

When the goalkeeper possession rule was altered several years ago (keepers were forced to use their hands less and their feet more), the "ideal" goalie switched almost overnight from a tall shot-stopper to a quick, agile athlete with excellent footwork.

Instill the Proper Athletic Values in Your Child It is easy for a youngster who receives adulation from adults to feel special—"better than" her less favored teammates. This is especially true when her coach tells everyone else on the field to pass her the ball all the time or when she is the girl constantly singled out for praise, asked for halftime comments, and handed awards. Parents can keep children's feet planted firmly on the ground by stressing the importance of teamwork and teammates. Do not miss any opportunity to praise the play of others on your child's squad. Give credit to the girl who passed your daughter the ball for the winning goal, or who played as hard defense as she could on the field for your spectacular goalkeeping child. So that the entire team can benefit from her skills, let your daughter know that it is her responsibility as a leading player to raise the play of others to her level.

Insist that Your Child Show Respect for the Coach It is easy to castigate a coach when a child knows more about the game than the coach apparently does. It is also counterproductive to the team and of course to the child himself. Youngsters should always be taught respect for adults. Beyond that, the coach might have some valuable things to impart about athletics in general, such as strategy and sportsmanship.

Continue to Challenge Your Child This does not mean pushing her; it does mean raising the bar so that she becomes neither complacent nor bored. It is easy for a youngster who is the team's standard-bearer to feel self-satisfied. However, that same child may very soon become an ex-player, or at least an ex-great player. Seek out competitive opportunities for your excellent athlete, from camps to travel experiences to simply trying a different position on the field. At the same time, make sure she continues to find soccer fun—so don't overdo any one thing.

Encourage Other Interests All soccer and no play makes Johnny a very dull boy. It also makes Johnny a candidate for misery when—whether at age fifteen, twenty-five, or fifty—he moves on to other things. Let him experiment with other sports if he wants to (or his friends do); let him also venture into other fields besides the athletic ones, such as music, Scouts, and (especially) academics. This last area is especially important, because . . .

College Soccer Scholarships Are No Sure Thing There are far fewer soccer scholarships available than most people realize. Chances are, soccer alone will not get your child into college; it is almost certain she will not get paid for her prowess. Brains are still the best route to higher education.

Maintain Your Own Perspective Don't become insufferable on the sidelines, in the supermarket, or at the community picnic. Not everyone cares about your child's latest exploits. Learn to give others a break—which means from time to time giving soccer a break.

THE LAST RESERVE

Much of what is written about youth soccer focuses on the top players—and that is where most coaches direct their attention too. Even this book assumes that your soccer-playing child is of at least average ability.

But what is it like to be the parent of the weakest player on a team? Understanding what goes on in the head of a child who plays poorly may help you handle that boy or girl's situation a bit better.

Handling the Less-than-Average Players

Poor Players Usually Know They Are It has become a self-fulfilling prophecy: Because no one expects her to play better, she does not try to. A coach who challenges her just as much as he does a stellar player—not with the same goals but with the same intensity—may be the first ever to reach that player. It's more difficult for a parent (just as it is more difficult for a parent than a coach to reach many children), but that does not mean a parent should not try.

A Poor Player May Be Used to Put-downs or Sarcastic Comments These comments from classmates, teammates, maybe even coaches and parents, may not be overt or even conscious. The lowest ranked player enters the field, and the bench erupts: "Go get 'em, Darin!" "Try for the hat trick!" "Hey, guys, look, *Darin*'s in!" Each time he touches the ball, his teammates react. They may not be behaving this way to make Darin feel bad, but the effect can be the same: Something unusual is happening, and everyone's attention is drawn to it. (To be effective, the encouragement should not be overdone.)

A Poor Player May Try to Attract Attention Feeling left out, she may become the team clown; she'll joke around, lighten things up, maybe even be the coach's foil. There is nothing wrong with this, provided it does not detract from the team's concentration and does not diminish the player's desire to improve herself.

Or the player may become the team toady, picking up the balls after practice, always volunteering to run lines or fetch the ball in the woods.

Footnotes

For what it's worth (and besides, you can't do anything about it now anyway): The Washington State Youth Soccer association found that youngsters born in the first three quarters of the year were represented far more frequently on premier league teams than those born in the fourth quarter.

It's nice to be helpful, but the more a player performs this role, the more she edges over the line from team member to manager. Everyone—the star as well as the least sub—should fetch balls and run lines.

There Are Reasons a Poor Player Does Not Perform as Well as a Good One Perhaps the weaker player is not as talented physically; he cannot kick a ball as far, or is not as fast, coordinated, or agile. He tries to measure up but simply cannot. Adults (parents as well as coaches) are advised to have different expectations for different players at different times. Praise should be awarded based on individual standards, not on some mythical standard of excellence only the naturally gifted can achieve.

The Poorer Player May Be Developmentally Behind His Teammates, Either Intellectually or Emotionally It is terribly frustrating for a child to listen to her coach talk, see all her teammates nod their heads, then go off and perform as expected—while feeling like the only one who doesn't understand or grasp a thing that was said. Some extra, one-on-one attention, right after the speech and just before the activity begins, can reduce a child's frustration.

The Last Reserve Might Feel Unmotivated to Improve Himself Perhaps it is because no one notices the improvement he has already made. Adults often succumb to the temptation to stash players in boxes, and then keep them there. There is no reason to believe the last reserve will always be that—but coaches and spectators tend to pay less attention to the changing abilities of a weaker player, because we don't really expect him to get as good as the others. But if every adult not only expects but also encourages the least player to shed that status, we can finally banish from everyone's mind the idea of a "last reserve."

CHAPTER 3

Being a Better Soccer Parent: The Do's and Don'ts

Being a supportive soccer parent involves more than simply signing waiver forms and fueling up the minivan for endless trips to innumerable fields in nameless towns and cities far, far from home.

THE SUPPORTIVE PARENT

There are many things you can do—without knowing diddly about the game—to help your child be both a better player and a happier one. Considered separately, they may seem minor; together, they can make a major difference in your son or daughter's experience of the game.

Ways to Become Supportive

The Most Important Question You Can Ask after a Match Is Not "Who Won?" It is "Did you have fun?" Winning should never be the yardstick by which a child measures his soccer experience—after all, good teams playing well do lose, poor teams playing poorly do win, and when you get right down to it, winning or losing is not the point of youth sports anyway. A good youth soccer program fosters individual

Footnotes

Several years ago in North Carolina, two teams played for the U-14 state championship. They battled to a 1–1 regulation time result, then continued on even terms through overtime. With penalty kicks looming—and just four seconds remaining on the clock—one final desperation shot won the game for the Winston-Salem Twins. The winners celebrated jubilantly; the Chapel Hill team—especially the goalkeeper, who had played a superb game—was understandably devastated.

At that moment, a North Carolina Youth Soccer Association official watching from the sidelines told the stunned Chapel Hill parents to reach out to their emotionally drained sons. "Go tell them you love them," he said. "They played their hearts out. They need you to tell them they're okay."

The Chapel Hill goalkeeper, far from the goal and his teammates, was alone in his own hell, blaming himself for his team's failure. Then, all of a sudden, the Twins' assistant coach walked slowly toward the keeper. As the rest of his team celebrated at midfield, the man went over to the heartbroken boy. They spoke a couple of words, and then hugged.

That caring and compassion—and respect for a young athlete's needs and abilities—are what youth soccer is all about.

self-esteem, personal growth, and enjoyment. A good parent lets a child know that, win or lose, his or her efforts are appreciated, and there's no disappointment in the child himself or herself. A child's worth bears no relationship to the outcome of a match. Fun and enjoyment are focused on—not scores.

If You Have Nothing Good to Say after a Game, Say Nothing But if you do feel compelled to say something, make it as innocuous as humanly possible: "I'm glad it was you guys kicking around in all that mud, not me!"

Resist Sounding Negative This is easier said than done, for sure. You can sympathize—"Boy, you must have felt awful when you missed that penalty kick"—but you must resist the temptation to add a snippy, "Of course, how can you expect to make penalty kicks? You never work on them in practice!"

Avoid Criticizing Your Child's Teammates Don't say, "Too bad. It was all Tommy's fault"—even if it was. The last thing your youngster needs to hear from you is criticism of a team member. Besides, how would you feel if you learned that a parent in another minivan was criticizing *your* child?

On the Way Home Ask, "What Did You Learn Today?" When you get home ask, "Can you show me?" This reinforces the coach's lesson for that particular day. It also emphasizes that learning is important. Plus it bolsters a child in recognizing, for perhaps the first time in his life, he knows about something that his parents don't.

Challenge, Don't Threaten Using fear as a motivator takes all the fun out of the game. While it may produce short-term results, it seldom works in the long run. So instead of threatening, "You better score today—you haven't gotten off a good shot in three games!" issue a strong, positive challenge: "I think you guys are about ready to start firing some good shots this afternoon!"

Be Aware of the Pygmalion Effect This phenomenon is named after the Greek king Pygmalion who fell in love with a statue he had sculpted, which eventually came to life as the woman of his dreams. The Pygmalion effect was clearly demonstrated in a case where physical education teachers were informed that a test had pinpointed certain youngsters who would perform unusually well physically. The youngsters had actually been selected at random; nevertheless, when they were measured several months later, they did test far better at sit-ups, push-ups, long jumps, and running than did a control group. The implications for youth soccer are obvious. If a parent expects improvement from a child—or maturation, or leadership, or whatever—that expectation somehow gets communicated to the child. The higher we set the bar, the higher our children tend to jump.

Help Your Child Prepare for Tryouts Open tryouts—putting oneself on the line in front of strangers and peers—can be a harrowing experience for a child. You can help your child attain a positive frame of mind by countering his fears beforehand. Have a reply ready in case he says, "Oh, there's so many good players here, I don't have a chance" or "I'll never make it. The coaches already know who they want." Make sure your child arrives on time, carrying all appropriate gear (including a pair of comfortable, well-broken-in shoes) and forms. And then vanish. That does not mean you must drive all the way home and back again; what it does mean is that you should not hover on the sidelines, assessing his every move. No one likes such pressure—not your child and not the adults who are evaluating him.

Help Your Child Learn Discipline by Getting Her to Games and Practices on Time Your child's commitment to soccer is only as strong as your own. A player will show up on time and be ready to play only if you are as enthusiastic about soccer as she is. Your coach will thank you, and your child will start the day on the right foot (so to speak). Oh, yes: Don't forget to arrive promptly for pickup too!

Help Your Child Prepare His Equipment Bag for Games Players should pack certain things in their soccer bag: ball, uniform (including extra socks—and don't forget soccer shoes and shin guards!), water bottle, extra money, and snacks. It is nice to prepare your child's soccer bag for him—but far better is teaching him how to do it himself. The game of soccer teaches children to be independent. Parents should reinforce, rather than contradict, that lesson.

Attend Matches Whether she says so or not, it means a lot to your child to know that you are there watching her play. But remember: Be positive, or remain mute.

Do Not Attend Practices This is your child's time. This is when he concentrates on learning, shares laughter with teammates, and feels free to run around, unencumbered by teachers, parents, and the tensions of everyday life. Let him have this time to himself. You don't need to share every waking moment of your child's life—and not watching him all the time makes matches that much more special.

Make Sure You Understand the Philosophy of the Team and/or the Mission of the Club or League If you believe that in youth sports every player should play at least half of each game, but the coach is out to win as many games and tournaments as possible, chances are, conflicts will arise sooner rather than later. Similarly, if you belong to the you're-only-as-good-as-your-last-game school, and the aim of your child's club is long-term development, you (and your child) will have difficulty understanding why the coach keeps putting so-and-so on the field or does not appear worried during the team's three-game losing streak.

Make Sure You Understand that Soccer Means Different Things to Youngsters Who Are Different Ages Between six and twelve, boys and girls venture for the first time into the sports world—but they love the process of playing more than the actual winning or losing of any particular game. Between twelve and fourteen, sports provides crucial identification for youngsters. The chance to say, "I am a Wrecker" (or whatever the name of their team is) means everything at this age. Then, between ages fourteen and eighteen, youngsters use sports to assert their independence. This is not always easy on a parent—but it is inevitable.

Ask Your Child What the Coach Expects from Her in the Upcoming Match Even if you have no clue what she is talking about, nod wisely and ask how she expects to achieve those goals.

Support the Coach, Even If that Means Disappointing Your Child Don't automatically agree, "Yes, that coach is an idiot for taking you out in the final ten minutes. How does he ever expect to win if you're not on the field?" You might use your child's disappointment to introduce a discussion of how to handle life's frustrations. Perhaps you can help your child see life from the point of view of a substitute who seldom plays but is always at practice and finally gets a chance. Or, if you don't know what to say, simply shut up and be ready to listen as your child works through things on his own.

Encourage Your Child to Communicate Directly with the Coach Don't allow yourself to be put in the position of middleman (or woman). You will do far more for your child by teaching him to speak and stand up for himself—and then allowing him to do so.

Prepare Nutritious Meals—Especially before Games Take a look at the chapter on "Eating Well" for specific information—you may be surprised how important nutrition is for young players. Whenever you send your child off to a game (or longer), make sure she has healthy foods with her to snack on.

Watch Soccer Videos, or Games on Television with Your Child Take her to professional, college, even high school games. Allow her to teach you about what you're seeing. For once, your child can act as the teacher, and you the pupil.

Encourage Your Child to Read about Positive Role Models in Soccer Each day more and more information is available: in books, magazines, and newspapers, as well as on the Internet. Providing your child with written material or showing him how to find it on the Web serves two purposes: It shows you're interested in his life, and it reinforces the value of the written word.

Never, Ever, Abuse a Referee, or Question a Call Of all the behaviors adults should model, this is among the most important. Right or wrong, an official's judgment must stand. So much that is wrong with professional sports today arises from abusive behavior toward referees —behavior that is allowed to fester, then erupts in potentially dangerous circumstances.

Praise Other Players Enough said.

Expect Your Child to Make Mistakes Soccer is a game of errors; the players who do best are those who accept that fact. They also learn from their mistakes and move on. Encourage your child not to dwell on slip-ups but instead to reflect on them toward figuring out what he might do differently. In the words of sports psychologist Alan Goldberg, "Give the gift of failure. The most successful athletes are willing to take more risks than others (and therefore fail more frequently); they also use their failures as a positive source of motivation and improvement. Teach your child to view setbacks and mistakes positively, and you'll give him the key to a lifetime of success."

Avoid Comparisons They are often inaccurate, generally useless, and always destructive, for one simple reason: Each child is unique. Each young soccer player has his or her own special strengths, weaknesses, motivations, fears, and most important, paths of physical and emotional development. In other words, each child matures and plays differently. Holding up another child as a model inhibits your son or daughter from developing his or her own unique set of skills.

Maintain Perspective Can you remember what you were like, physically and emotionally, at your child's age? Do you recall what you were capable of accomplishing and what you found impossible to achieve? Think back to what you talked about with your parents and what kinds of things you would never have discussed with them then. Soccer is a wonderful vehicle for communicating with your child, but it cannot magically open age-inappropriate doors.

Try Not to Overanalyze Each Game or Your Youngster's Performance in It The true "winner" in soccer is the player who leaves the field proud of what he did well, regardless of the outcome. The final score is not a reliable indicator of your child's happiness or satisfaction with soccer.

Teach Your Child Never to View His Opponent as "The Bad Guy," or Some Faceless Nonentity Don't demonize other players, teams, or coaches. Instead, guide your child in relating to them in human terms. Never gloat over the opposing team's slip-ups, such as missed penalty kicks. There's a way of teaching your child to be a poor winner just as there is of teaching him to be a poor loser.

Be Honest with Yourself about Your Child Realistically assess your child's athletic ability, skill levels, competitive attitude, and sportsmanship. If you cannot view your child objectively, chances are, you cannot judge the soccer team, league, season, or program objectively either.

Learn the Rules of the Game Don't guess. If you understand what you're watching, you'll get a lot more out of the time you spend on the sidelines. You'll also be able to have lots more intelligent conversations with your child—about something she loves. (For general information on rules of the game, see "The Basics" section in this book. For more detailed information, take a refereeing course!)

Don't be Afraid to Kick the Ball Around with Your Child Do this no matter how great the disparity between his skills and yours. In fact, a youngster's confidence soars when she realizes she can do things a parent can't. Plus, asking her to teach something helps her become a better player.

Think of Ways to Help Your Child Practice at Home Toss balls to help him practice control. Set up a backyard obstacle course, including cones to dribble around, a bench placed on its side for *wall passes,* and tires to jump through for agility. Set aside an area for shooting, and rig up a goal using an old net and a couple of trees. But beware: That patch of lawn won't stay green for long. And it just might become the most popular spot in the neighborhood.

Send Him to Soccer Camp A week's worth of expert instruction, fun practice, and lively competition can do wonders. (And believe it or not, most youngsters relish the chance to get away from home!)

Buy Her Two Balls One should be a quality, stitched ball to use on grass; the other a cheaper, laminated one to kick on concrete or against a wall for practice. You might also donate a soccer ball to your child's school. It's amazing how many games occur spontaneously at recess or lunch when a ball happens to be nearby.

Don't Assume That Just Because You're Freezing on the Sidelines, Your Child Is Also Cold Players might feel cold at first; they warm up quickly, however, once they start playing. That's why they're better off not bundled up like soccer-playing Eskimos. And keep in mind: As soon as an overdressed player stops playing, she risks chills from sweaty clothing.

Remember That Soccer Is Your Child's Game, Not Yours If your son or daughter is playing soccer in order to please you, everyone ultimately loses. Resist laying guilt trips on your youngster: "We've spent so much on soccer already, you better keep playing." They seldom work, and they always come back to haunt you.

Never Take Away Your Child's Dreams You can smile inwardly when your daughter says her ambition is to play in the Olympics, or your son announces he's going be in the 2010 World Cup, but don't laugh out loud. Every child needs to dream—and besides, *someone* has to be in the Olympics and the World Cup. Why not him or her?

Recognize That as the Parent of a Young Soccer Player, You Take on Many Roles At various times, you will serve as a doctor, chauffeur, tailor, shoemaker, masseur (or masseuse), nutritionist, travel consultant, telephone receptionist, physical therapist, and newspaper clipping service. You will be expected to run a lost-and-found bureau, along with a twenty-four-hour-a-day cafeteria. It's a tall order—but also an opportunity to involve yourself with your child in an activity he or she loves. The alternative is to shut yourself out of a big part of your child's life—and that is no real alternative at all.

Your Child's Performance Does Not Reflect on His Worth—or Yours In other words, his self-worth has nothing to do with the number of goals he scores or how many saves he makes. If your child happens to shank an easy shot, or let in an easy goal, that has nothing to do with how good a human being he is—and even less to do with you, your skills as a parent, and your standing among friends, neighbors, and relatives. Why react with disgust or anger.

Finally, If You're Really Into It, Become a Volunteer Coach, or Even a Referee A special parenting issue arises when a father or mother coaches his or her own child. There are two major pitfalls: The parent favors the child, either consciously or unconsciously, or the parent overcompensates and treats the child tougher than anyone else on the team.

Parents who coach their own child should:

➤ *Talk with the youngster before the season begins.* The parent should stress his or her responsibility as a coach, as opposed to his or responsibility as a mom or dad, and discuss the difficulties of being objective. The parent might ask for suggestions from the child and from other family members as well.

➤ *Use objective measures to help evaluate all team members.* Soccer is not big on statistics, but speed, goals for and against, and fouls can all be quantified. The more objective measures a parent/coach uses, the more fairly he or she can decide when, where, and for how long a son or daughter should play.

➤ *Ask a trusted friend to observe practices and games.* This friend can provide valuable input as to how fairly the parent/coach is treating everyone on the team.

THE FINE ART OF SPECTATING

Watching soccer involves far more than simply screaming at Brianna-Lu to belt the ball downfield (or, alternatively, screaming at the other team for simply belting the ball downfield and not playing real soccer). Watching soccer is an art. Yet unlike most art, one need not be exceptionally trained or skilled—or lucky—to be a success. It does not take much for parents to become good spectators, even if they don't know a shin guard from a throw-in.

Be a Good Spectator

Come Prepared You'll enjoy the game more if you're armed with all the essentials: sunscreen, mittens, umbrellas, hats (for both heat and cold), parkas, blankets, and lawn chairs.

Show Support for Everyone on Your Child's Team That includes reserves as well as starters. Don't open your newspaper the moment the subs are sent in or as soon as Jeffrey Jr. comes out. There are eleven players on the field, not one. (Actually, there are twenty-two, counting the other team. And don't forget the referee—she deserves a bit of recognition too.)

Applaud Good Plays by Either Team It takes no more effort to cheer a great save by the other team's goalkeeper than it does to clap for "the good guy."

Don't Shout Instructions from the Sidelines Whether your words of advice are brilliant or idiotic is immaterial; the point here is simply that you must stifle the urge to say anything that hints of coaching. Competing voices (from the sidelines) make it difficult for your child to hear those that really count: his coach's and his teammates'. Conflicting advice puts your child in the wrenchingly difficult situation of asking, "Whose words matter most?" Plus the whole idea of playing soccer is to learn to think and act for yourself. Telling a child what to do every time the ball comes near him is counterproductive to his development as a soccer player. He does not need you to tell him where to kick the ball, what part of his body to use, and where to run next. In fact, you are the *last* person on earth who should be giving such advice.

This does not mean you must remain silent; what it does mean is that you should limit your comments to simple slogans of praise such

Footnotes

Concerned that adults were becoming overly involved in youth soccer games, coaches of two U-10 teams in Wisconsin devised an experiment. They divided the game into four quarters, rather than two halves. During the first and third quarters, coaches and parents promised to say only things like "Nice job," "Way to go," and "Good!" In the second and fourth quarters, however, they would be allowed their "normal sideline behavior."

During the first quarter, the teams played well. They passed to open teammates, used open space intelligently, and defended strongly.

With the second period—and yelling from the sidelines—players became timid and reacted slowly. They stopped helping each other out verbally. They also stopped smiling.

In the third quarter, the game became fun again. Goals were scored and saved. Players left the field laughing.

The fourth quarter brought more yelling and again, a change in the style of play. Talk among players was less positive and more critical. When the final whistle blew, players didn't appear happy they had played a match.

as, "Nice pass!" "Great shot!" and "Ooooh, s-o-o-o close!" (Note that those words come *after* a play, not during it.)

Soccer Players Always Have Several Options Some options are better than others, but none is rarely the only right one. Soccer is all about learning which option to choose and when. Professional players don't always make the right choices—World Cup games are full of bone-headed decisions—so why expect perfection from the very young? Instead, praise the decisions they do make (on their own!). When they try to do the right thing but it doesn't work, yell, "Good idea!"

Consider Not Yelling at All Try it some time; you might be surprised at the positive effect this has on your child's game—and your own enjoyment of it.

Afraid you'd go crazy with nothing to do? Worried that silence conveys disinterest? Here are a few things to occupy your time:

> ➤ *Keep statistics (shots taken, passes attempted, passes completed, good defensive plays, etc.).* If you don't know what kind of statistics to record, be creative!
> ➤ *Get to know the other parents.* Talk to them. Point out what their children are doing well. Gossip (but not about soccer!).
> ➤ *Take pictures.* They make great gifts, especially when enlarged and distributed at a postseason banquet or party.

Don't Even Shout the Name of a Player This goes for your own child and everyone else's. Instead of yelling, "Attagirl, Terri Lynn! Way to crunch her!" you can encourage your daughter—and encourage team play for everyone—by cheering generically: "Go, Big Blue!"

Learn the Rules There is no more excruciating embarrassment for a child than a parent who shrieks for an offside call when the ball has yet to be played over the midfield line. (If you don't know why that's not offside, turn directly to "The Basics" section of this book.) Ignorance of the law—in this case, the law of the game—is no excuse.

Footnotes

It took just two games for a youth soccer coach in Ohio to get fed up with parental screaming from the sidelines. So he did what many coaches dream of doing: He scheduled a practice match for parents only.

The parents' performance was appalling. Mothers and fathers miskicked the ball. Their passes ran straight out of bounds. They bunched up, ran around aimlessly, and by halftime were so exhausted they could barely move.

Immediately the coach lit into them. "Don't bunch!" he yelled. "Run harder! Pass the ball to somebody!" These were exactly the words the parents had screamed from the sidelines.

The parents got the message. For the rest of the season they applauded every effort, regardless of the result. Their remarks consisted of "Nice try!" "Good effort!" "What a pass!"

The results were noticeable. The team played better (and won most of the time). And eight years later, it had the most number of original players of any team in the league.

Learn the Game Share books and videos with your child. Attend a coaching clinic, if only to find out what the coach goes through. Kick the ball around with your youngster in the backyard to learn how tough it is to make the ball do exactly what you want. Talk about the game whenever you get a chance: with your child, your child's friends, and other parents on the team.

Study Players' Technique For example, when a high ball comes out of the air, watch how players prepare to receive it, how quickly they decide which part of their body to use to control it, how they position their hands for balance, and what they do about opponents who are trying to get good position themselves. Plan to concentrate on only one or two technical skills—for example, making long passes and heading. Anticipate when those skills will be used during a match; once they are, try to block everything else from your mind.

Study One Player Throughout the Match Select someone who plays the same position as your child; watch him with the ball as well as without it (this is called playing off the ball). See if you can figure out what he does well and what he does poorly. Is he magic with his right foot but seems never to use his left? Does he head well when unencumbered by others in the field, but refuse to challenge on high balls in crowds? Does he take a brief well-considered rest when he knows he won't be involved in a play, or does he race around the field like a headless chicken, tiring himself needlessly?

Tactics Are as Important as Technique The key to observing tactics is not to keep your eye on the ball. In fact, watch everything *but* the ball. Choose a spot on the field well away from where the action is. Watch a player on the attacking team lull her defender into a false sense of security, then suddenly sprint into open space. Or check out a defensive midfielder as she marks her man, then races into the penalty area to cover up a teammate's mistake. Ask yourself, "How did those players figure out what was going to happen before it did?" See if you can anticipate a similar situation.

Team Strategy Can Be Easily Analyzed Try to figure out what formation each team uses (in other words, how many defenders, midfielders, and forwards they have). Check from time to time throughout the game to see if anything has changed. Watch how both sides set up for and react to set plays (free kicks, corner kicks, goal kicks). Analyze what a team does when they are down by a goal late in the game; try to determine if they play differently from when they began. You won't always know all the answers—but your analysis can initiate interesting conversations on the sideline.

Try to Get a Feel for the Pace of a Game Every match is played at a different tempo. So, too, does the pace change during a game. Sometimes every player seems to be active; at other times, only two or three are clearly in motion. See if you can understand why the tempo changes, and try to figure out when it will change next.

Seek out Players after the Match Say something personal to them. This includes athletes on the opposing team as well as their coaches and parents. Everyone likes to hear compliments. It need not be for a spectacular game—"Great clear at the end, Emily" or "Boy, Coach, your team is really tough to beat!" can work wonders. If you can't find something intelligent to say about the game, try this: "You really looked like you were having fun out there." The idea is to acknowledge the play and not the final score.

Don't Forget to Say Something Positive to Your Own Child Yes, even if he scored the own goal (a goal that the defender inadvertently puts into his own net, by mistake), or was out on the field for just the final few minutes. Let him know you were not only physically present at the game, but you were watching it as well.

Know When to Shut Up as Well as When to Yell No comment is necessary when one player deliberately fouls another, for example—and that goes for the parents of both the fouler and the foulee.

Let the Referee Referee Most referees are young, and still learning their craft. One of the referee's many jobs it to help teach the youngsters on the field about sportsmanship, fair play, and the spirit of the game. Allow them to do that without interference. Their decisions are final. Disputing a call never changes it; it just distracts the players and the flow of the game.

And by the way: When the assistant referee asks you to please get off the (literal) sideline, do so! Players have the right to cross the line to try to keep a ball in play, and they cannot if spectators are in the way. Also, linesmen need an unobstructed view of the sideline to determine whether a ball is in or out of play. And, of course, in the United States there is always the question of legal liability whenever a player or referee bangs into a spectator.

Get to Know the Other Folks on the Sidelines And once you have made the acquaintance of these folks, do not undermine through name-calling, backbiting, or idle gossip the team concept the coach is trying to build. (This also goes for what you say at home and in the carpool van. Just because a comment is made away from the field does not mean it is any less powerful.) And remember: The "folks on the sidelines" includes parents from the opposition. They're not from some alien planet; they have children (and feelings) too.

Ask the Coach and Manager What You Can Do to Make Their Jobs Easier It doesn't take a soccer genius to volunteer to drive, bring water, make phone calls, or arrange a post-season party. All it takes is enthusiasm, time, and effort.

Don't Overanalyze Each Match or Your Youngster's Performance in It The true "winner" in soccer is the young player who leaves the field proud he did the best he was capable of, regardless of the outcome. The final score should not be the sole guide of your child's happiness and satisfaction with soccer. If you ask, "What did you like about today's game?" (as opposed to "So, what about that point spread?") you may be surprised at the variety of answers you'll hear—and the breadth and depth of the conversation that ensues.

No Swearing or Incendiary Comments These are out of place at any event involving young people, whether it's a youth soccer match or a family reunion. Hearing such remarks from adults on the sidelines communicates to the youngsters that this kind of language is acceptable in public situations. Is that the message you want to send?

Remember That Soccer Is Only a Game When your team is on top, realize it was not always that way—nor will it always be. When things are going less successfully, remember the same thing. Focus on the beauty, grace, and harmony of the game rather than on the final score. Soccer is a wonderful sport—even more so when played without interference from the sidelines.

OVERINVOLVEMENT

Overinvolvement—a polite word for "obsessive behavior"—is a common trait in parents of youth soccer players. While taking an interest in your child's experience with soccer is good—even desirable—there is a distinct line between encouragement and fanaticism.

The signs of overinvolvement are legion. They include focusing too much on the outcome of individual games, rather than on overall skill development, enjoyment, and the accomplishment of long-term goals; shouting from the sidelines at players, coaches, and referees; worrying intensely about coaches' decisions and talking at length to him or her about them; getting into game-related arguments with other parents (from your own team as well as the opposition); constantly comparing your child with others; punishing your child for not performing well or failing to meet your standards; forcing your child to practice at home; and continually raising the topics of college athletic scholarships with your child. A good clue that you are overinvolved is that your child says he no longer enjoys soccer; another is that she asks you to stop attending games.

Why Parents Become Too Involved

They Lack Experience with the Game They have no first-hand sense of the creativity needed to play the game—much less the freedom a boy or girl feels during a match, whether it's the league championship or a short-sided scrimmage. What to do? Get kicking yourself. Try a game with both adult and child players. Once parents have experienced the sport themselves—and learned the hard way that it's not as easy as it looks to make the ball do just what you want it to—then their overbearing behavior might decrease.

They View Their Child's Accomplishments as Their Own If Lance is not going to be the baseball star Dad never was, then he might as well be the soccer star Dad never even dreamed of being. But maybe Lance is the kind of kid who does not live for soccer; he likes it well enough, but it is not the all-consuming passion it must be if he is to become a star. Dad needs to "grow up" and learn to accept that.

Footnotes

A survey revealed that a sizable chunk—25 percent—of parents care whether their children win or lose at team sports. Thirty percent reward their children when they lose; 40 percent do so when they win. Thirty percent feel they could "at least sometimes" do a better job than a coach, while 45 percent believe they could do a better job than the referee. In addition, 10 percent admitted to yelling at coaches or referees (the actual figure is thought to be 40 to 50 percent).

Nearly 50 percent of all parents "almost always feel as though they are competing in the game when they watch their children compete." While parents feel a similar investment in their offspring no matter what the activity—music, drama, debating—sports events allow spectators to be more vocal in their participation. They can cheer wildly or protest loudly—and such behavior is socially acceptable and even encouraged.

They Carry the Old "Kill the Ump!" Mentality with Them to the Soccer Field Parents harassing soccer officials—especially when those parents are not always certain about what constitutes a hand ball, offside, advantage, or even a direct kick—is inexcusable. In soccer, one team inevitably wins and the other loses. Assigning blame won't change that, it only wastes time and energy. Furthermore, youngsters who hear their parents toss blame around like so many throw-ins learn the wrong lesson. A solution to this problem is to follow the lead of those leagues and associations that require every parent to take his or her turn with the whistle (after proper training, of course).

It Stems from Their Own Competitive Nature Americans are brought up to believe that winning is the only reason to play sports; if you're not number one, you're number zero; a winner never quits and a quitter never wins, and yada yada yada. While winning is good, it is *not* the be-all and end-all—nor is it the sole reason youngsters play sports. A recent survey of 10,000 young people between the ages of ten and eighteen asked why they enjoyed athletics. "Winning" was far down the list, coming in tenth place—well behind "having fun" (number one) and "improving skills" (number two). Parents who get caught up in the competitive aspect of soccer tend not only to miss the real benefits of the game but to rob their child of those benefits as well.

Some Parents Become Overinvolved Because They See Soccer as a Way for Them to Look Good In many communities, soccer is the major youth sport; successful players are well-known, and their parents bask in the same warm glow. But of course, children should not be made to bear responsibility for their parents' reputations.

What Can You Do if You Suspect Yourself of Edging Toward Over-involvement? First check to see how wrapped up you are in youth soccer; next assess your reasons for feeling as strongly as you do about what is really only a game; then back off. Lessen your commitment; cut down on the hours you spend on the sidelines. Your enthusiasm for the game does not have to diminish; however, the way you express that enthusiasm does.

Chances are you'll find yourself enjoying youth soccer more than ever, once you are able to step back and view it from a healthy distance. And, speaking of health, chances are your blood pressure will go down too!

VOLUNTEERING

You may be a soccer novice—in fact, you might not be able to tell the difference between a soccer ball, a golf ball, or the Inaugural Ball—but that does not mean you can't contribute to the game.

Volunteer positions abound in youth soccer. World Cup-style knowledge is not a requirement; time, enthusiasm, and skill or expertise in a particular area are.

What can *you* do?

Become an Administrator
If you have organizational skills—the ability to put together schedules, delegate responsibility, meet deadlines, and make things happen—and if you enjoy crossing every *t* and dotting every *i*, then administration is for you. The world of youth soccer is desperate for treasurers, secretaries, field supervisors, tournament directors, league presidents, division coordinators, referee schedulers, and the like. In fact, if you're any good at all as an administrator, before you know it you'll be a president, chairperson—or soccer czar.

Become a Fund-raiser
The universe is divided into two types of people: those who like asking for money and those who don't. If you're in the former group,

F o o t n o t e s

If you're going to wash cars for a fund-raiser, you might as well do it right. Several years ago, Connecticut's Westport Strikers U-13 boys team wanted to raise money for a trip to England, Holland, and Germany. They got the following idea from a New Jersey club and improved on it.

This was no ordinary car wash. First the boys spent weeks canvassing the town for pledges. Townspeople agreed to donate 5, 10, or 25 cents per total number of cars washed. Anyone who pledged received a coupon for a free wash.

The car wash itself took place on a Sunday at a clothing store parking lot donated by one of the fathers—a spot with high visibility in town. A policeman directed traffic as music blared from powerful speakers to further attract patrons.

As drivers (without coupons) entered, they were asked to pay $3 minimum, and most donated more as requested. Children in cars were handed free balloons and candy; adults were presented with a printed handout, including infor-mation about the car wash, histories of both the team and the Westport Soccer Association, and a team photo.

There were five washing stations, all manned by parents, players, and siblings. Sawhorses controlled the traffic flow. As each driver left (sparkling clean), a large "tote board" at the exit kept a running count of the number of cars served.

Between 9 A.M. and 5 P.M.—aided by beautiful spring weather—the Strikers and their helpers washed 538 cars. That brought in several thousand dollars. When the pledges were collected (those who pledged were offered a chance to "downsize," based on the enormous number of cars), the team raised nearly $30,000.

Part of the money paid for a well-deserved pizza party. The rest paid for an even more well-deserved trip to Europe.

fund-raising is for you. There are thousands of ways to raise cash, ranging from finding sponsors to organizing tournaments to selling goods and services to running special events. You don't need to know what makes a soccer field green; you do need to know how to fill your treasury so it turns that color.

Work on Publicity

If you like to work with words, or have experience in the media, this job is for you. Between writing up game results, feature stories, upcoming events and calendars, promotions, and the like, you'll have your computer working full time. And speaking of things high tech . . .

Work on a Web Site

Every youth soccer club worth its gigabytes now has a home page. If you're a skillful "surfer," volunteer to create, improve, or maintain your club's Internet presence. There's no telling where a soccer club will land once it leaps into cyberspace, but the trip is sure to be interesting.

Offer to Assist the Coach

Varsity coaches are often overwhelmed with duties. Perhaps there is a scholarship fund that needs attending to, an alumni tournament that needs organizing, a newsletter that needs sending, a trophy case that needs maintaining, an end-of-season banquet that needs planning, or a civic meeting about a playing field that needs packing with parental supporters. Whatever the task, the coach can't do it alone.

Run a Reality Check

Your time is precious; in order not to get boxed into a commitment you can't fulfill, you should ask yourself the following questions:

➤ *Is this an organization I feel comfortable working with?* Do I support its mission and philosophy? Is it a group I am proud (or at least not ashamed) to be associated with publicly?

➤ *Do I really have the time and energy this work demands?* Make sure the position you're applying for (or have been asked to fill) has been fully explained, in terms of job description, expectations, work load, and available support.

➤ *Am I willing to take responsibility for my decisions?* You might be asked to take controversial stands regarding personnel, money expenditures, team decisions, or political issues. Some people are unwilling to sit on the hot seat; others relish it.

➤ *Do I have a habit of overcommitting myself, making promises I find difficult to keep?* Some folks just can't say no.

➤ *Am I willing to back my organization in public, even if I don't agree with its every decision?* Sometimes an organization takes a stand that every member does not support. For the ultimate good of the group, dirty laundry must not be aired in public.

➤ *Am I interested enough in what I'm doing to make the effort to learn to do it better?* Some folks are eager to take on new challenges; others simply cannot commit to the long learning curve certain jobs require.

➤ *Am I a willing subordinate?* Some folks just don't do well with bosses.

➤ *Am I able to delegate responsibility?* If you are asked to fill a managerial post, you need to be able to assign tasks to others. Trying to do everything yourself is a certain prescription for burnout (see section on "Burnouts and Dropouts").

➢ *Does it matter that I might work many hours and make many sacrifices doing a job that few people will appreciate or even notice?* If you're looking for glory, being a youth soccer volunteer is not how to find it. The only ones involved in the sport who should get their names in the paper are the players. If the reason you want to volunteer is for fame and fortune, find another group!

CHAPTER 4
Health Watch

E very youth soccer parent should know how to evaluate a child's injury. While major injuries will obviously be handled by coaches and trained medical personnel, parents need to be able to deal with minor problems that inevitably pop up. Young players need reassurance they'll be okay; parents need reassurance they won't have to run to the orthopedist or emergency room every time their child limps home from the field. Parents also need to understand that once an injury occurs, a child should not return to soccer until fully healed— meaning pain-free, with full motion and strength in the injured area, and willing to begin playing again.

INJURIES AND AILMENTS

There are various ailments parents should be aware of.

Blisters
Though seemingly minor, these can be quite a pain in the butt (though of course we're talking about the ones on the foot). Blisters develop

from excessive friction, often from new shoes. Consequently, new soccer shoes should be worn around the house or yard for a couple of days
to break them in before playing in them. Blisters can be prevented by
applying foot powder, wearing two pairs of socks, or rubbing petroleum jelly outside the sock or inside the shoe at the spot where friction
will most likely occur. When blisters do appear, they should be allowed
to heal on their own. Meanwhile, covering the blister with a dough-
nut-shaped pad helps keep painful pressure off it. If a blister pops, it
should be cleaned thoroughly and covered with a bandage.

Raspberries or Strawberries

Known to another generation as abrasions or scrapes, these raw red
marks come from too much slide-tackling. They should be washed
with clean water, then covered with an antibiotic ointment or powder.
During play, they should be covered with a nonsticking gauze, then
wrapped with a gauze or ace bandage. When the player is idle, the
wound should be left open to the air to dry.

Blood Clots under the Toenail

These usually involve the big toe and can be quite painful. Using a
paper clip (after the outer end has been placed in the center of a
match flame until the metal glows) to bore a hole in the nail bed
allows blood to escape from underneath, relieves pain, prevents infec-
tion, and facilitates early recovery. Ice should be applied to minimize
pain; antibiotic ointment, elevation, rest, and pain relievers complete
the therapy.

Athlete's Foot

Prevention is the best cure. Players should use shower slippers, and
should avoid wearing teammates' shoes and socks. Socks should be

changed daily. Treatment for athlete's foot includes keeping the feet dry and clean and using antifungal powder or cream.

Shin Splints

Though shin splints are one of the most common soccer injuries, many parents and coaches know little about them. Symptoms include burning or persistent pain and tenderness near the shins. Shin splints often occur after a sudden increase in running and kicking during the first days or weeks of a new season. They can also be caused by playing on a hard surface, wearing poorly cushioned shoes, or using poor running technique. Rest and ice help reduce the soft-tissue inflammation; changing to a well-padded soccer shoe, or one with more cleats, also works. Anti-inflammatory medication and aspirin diminish the pain. Ice should be applied in fifteen to twenty minute increments; heat therapy of any kind should be avoided. Athletes with shin splints should avoid jumping exercises and should rest as much as possible.

Rehabilitation includes toe raises (standing with toes on the ground, and slowly raising and lowering the heels). Athletes susceptible to shin splints should stretch the calf and shin regions prior to every practice and game. Also, lower legs can be strengthened by walking on the heels, toes, and outsides and insides of the ankles.

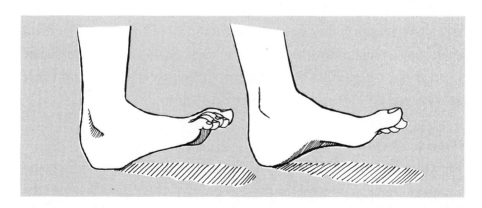

Ankle Sprain

This occurs most frequently when the ankle turns awkwardly on a rough spot on the field or during contact. The best treatment is RICE: Rest, Ice, Compression (wrapping the ice in an elastic bandage and pressing it against the injury), and Elevation. After an ankle sprain heals, many athletes subconsciously favor the injured side; that, along with less flexible calves and Achilles tendons because of inactivity, often leads to minor pain either right behind the heel or to the sides of the heel, near the bottom of the foot.

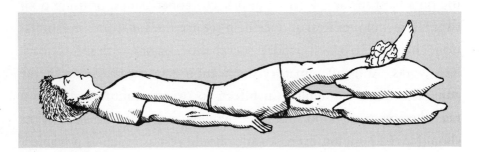

Heel Pain

The onset of this pain, which often coincides with the onset of puberty, is most common in males. Ice helps; so does moist heat in the form of whirlpools or hot soaks. Stretching and limiting the amount of running done each day is also beneficial. However, the most effective pain management technique is wearing well-padded shoes in combination with rubber heel cups. Studded shoes should be avoided during episodes of acute pain. Achilles heel pain should never be ignored; tight tendons can eventually rupture.

Knee Pain

This can be caused by an injury involving twisting of the leg, by rough impact, or by weak quadricep muscles that allow the kneecap to slide to the side and strain the joint. (Female players are more prone to knee injuries than are males, because their knees have a smaller bone structure, and there's less muscle mass around the joint as well as a looser arrangement of supporting ligaments.) Playing when experiencing knee pain can cause an athlete to limp, which can lead to bursitis and hip pain. Knee pain should not be self-treated. Sports doctors can prescribe strengthening exercises as well as orthotics for shoes.

To prevent knee pain many experts advise athletes to strengthen the knee area. Strong quadriceps, calves, and ankles take pressure off the knee. A regular strengthening program is recommended, including isometrics (contracting specific muscles against an immovable force), leg raises (sometimes with light weights strapped around the ankle or foot), toe raises, sit-ups, and other exercises (including, for girls, exercises to strengthen the inner thigh). Swimming and bicycling can also help strengthen weak knees. A sports doctor, trainer, or physical therapist can suggest specific exercises.

Exercises to avoid include step aerobics, squats, and deep knee bends.

Hamstring Pull

Soccer players are particularly susceptible to pulls or tears of this muscle in the back of the thigh. Such injuries, which can be very painful, take a while to heal. Rest is important. Stretching is effective in developing strong hamstrings, and preventing pulls.

Groin Pull

This common soccer injury results when a player reaches or lunges for a ball just out of reach. It can also occur during run-of-the-mill game situations, such as goal kicks or sliding tackles. As with hamstring pulls, stretching is a good preventive measure.

Stress Fractures

These occur when an athlete engages in vigorous repetitive activity; the increased muscle tension puts stress on certain bones, particularly those not yet fully developed. Stress fractures can occur in athletes who have played soccer for years. Players are particularly vulnerable during training sessions, before the regular season begins. Parts of the foot may not be able to handle the sudden transition to running hard, stopping and turning suddenly, and kicking balls on hard surfaces.

Symptoms of stress fractures include local pain, tenderness, and perhaps some swelling, all aggravated by motion and weight bearing. It is important to note that the fracture may not show up at all on an X-ray. Because the bone is not fully broken, there is no fracture line or large bone fragments. Instead, the fibers in the bone itself have been stressed or cracked and are attempting to heal themselves. Treatment depends on the bone involved, the severity of pain, and the degree to which the injury limits participation. Rest is the most common treatment for stress fractures, although a cast may be prescribed for additional support or relief of pain.

Lower Back Pain

This is more common in soccer players than one might imagine. It is often a function of tight hamstrings, which cause the hips to tilt. Athletes with lower-back pain should strengthen their abdominal muscles by doing crunches. In addition, they should stretch the back and hamstrings well, in order to prevent further back injuries such as a herniated disk or pinched nerve.

Dehydration

Most soccer players do not drink nearly enough water (or sports drinks). Players should take liquids before, during, and after training and games. They should not wait until they are thirsty. By then it is too late.

Footnotes

Several years ago, a youth coach was walking between two of the thirty fields used at a 6-on-6 tournament. Some of the fields were empty; on one, youngsters were kicking balls around for fun.

One shot soared over the goal and struck the coach. He fell into the goalpost, hit his head, and, according to the subsequent lawsuit, was unable to hold a job or "pursue many of the functions of a normal adult."

He sued the tournament for $675,000, claiming that officials should have supervised the youngsters better and that fans should have been kept 80 feet from each field to ensure their safety. The defense argued that supervision was above average (there were three police officers on duty) and that as an experienced coach, the plaintiff should have been aware of the danger of errant soccer balls.

After a four-day trial, a jury found in favor of the tournament.

The motto: At a soccer match, watch where you're walking; some balls don't always go where you think they will.

Sunburn

Cool compresses and an emollient or over-the-counter hydrocortisone lotion help soothe the skin. Severe sunburn should be seen by a dermatologist. One bad sunburn suffered as a child can result in skin cancer decades later.

Players should use sunscreen (preferably with an SPF of 15 or greater) and wear hats as much as possible. Sunscreen should be applied liberally, even on cloudy or hazy days, and especially on players scrimmaging as skins (players who take off their shirts in a scrimmage). All players should be encouraged to seek shade wherever possible (peak sun damage occurs between 10 A.M. and 3 P.M.) One league in Georgia even planted shade trees near their playing fields and erected shelters over team benches.

Concussions

Though not common, concussions are possible in any sport. Contrary to popular belief, heading a soccer ball incorrectly will not cause a concussion; however, two players going for a head ball can clunk heads, and a concussion may result. General signs and symptoms of concussions include unconsciousness, amnesia, disorientation, dilation of one or both pupils, nausea or vomiting, seeing spots, or hearing ringing sounds.

Concussions are classified into three degrees. A first degree (mild) concussion may not involve any loss of consciousness or coordination. There may be temporary confusion, with some memory loss or dizziness, and recovery is usually rapid. A player with a first-degree concussion can return to action after being evaluated by a physician; the major determinant is the severity of the headache.

A second-degree (moderate) concussion may involve loss of consciousness for three or four minutes, worsening amnesia, confusion, dizziness and ringing in the ears, and unsteadiness. Recovery takes several minutes. A second-degree concussion requires closer physical evaluation than does a first degree concussion before the player can resume soccer.

A third-degree (severe) concussion may involve loss of consciousness for five or more minutes as well as confusion, worsening amnesia, dizziness and ringing in the ears, and marked unsteadiness. Hospitalization may be required, and the recovery rate is slow.

Nosebleeds

A common soccer injury, a nosebleed can mask a broken nose (which is often indicated by breathing difficulties or swelling). The best first aid for a nosebleed is to place a small bag of ice on the bridge of the nose. Rolled gauze strips can be used to plug the nostril. A player with a nosebleed should not lean the head back; this causes blood to leak from the sinus cavities into the stomach.

Teeth Injuries

When a tooth is knocked out, make an effort to find it quickly so that a dentist can remount it. Once found, it should not be handled by the root. Use water to clean the tooth of dirt and debris. It should be kept wet and transported to the dentist in sterile, moist gauze or in a cup of water.

Asthma

More and more young soccer players (and children in general) suffer from asthma. Certain asthma is exercise induced—the smooth muscles of the lungs and airways constrict and hamper breathing, perhaps because of the increased air intake that occurs during physical exertion—but asthma need not prevent a child from playing soccer. Some tips are:

> ➤ The coach should be alerted to the problem.
> ➤ The child should take any necessary medication twenty minutes before beginning training or games. Over-the-counter drugs are not recommended; they are effective for only fifteen minutes and may produce such side effects as increased heart rate.

➢ An inhaler may be needed in cool weather. It should be kept in a warm spot, such as a coach or parent's pocket, not left on the sidelines in a soccer bag.

➢ An asthmatic child should drink plenty of water before, during, and especially after a game. Moisture helps keep airways open.

➢ A solid twenty-minute warm-up session before the game allows the child time to get used to exercising and ensures that he or she is ready to play.

➢ Most important, asthmatics need frequent rest periods, "breathers." They should not play for long periods of time.

DEALING WITH ANXIETY

Though most youngsters enjoy soccer, others find it extremely stressful. The hours before a match—even a practice—can create intense anxiety in boys and girls for a variety of reasons. Some children may be ultra competitive and work themselves into anxious states of anticipation. Others may feel inadequate or inferior. Still others may have difficulty relating to teammates or fear coaches or adult spectators on the sidelines.

Yet whether expressed as muscle tension, butterflies, cotton mouth, irritability, or self-defeating thoughts, anxiety is no fun. It is also not easy to overcome. However, parents can help young athletes handle anxiety in a variety of ways.

Downplay Competition

Instead of the outcome of a match—"Boy, you guys better win today, or you'll never get into the playoffs!"—try placing the focus elsewhere.

Commenting, "You've been practicing great all week, haven't you?" is one way to instill a positive attitude without mentioning winning or losing. So is the casual remark "What a beautiful day to play!"

Talk About Anxiety

If your child seems unusually nervous, initiate a conversation about it. Share your own experiences with anxiety. Emphasize the futility of focusing on "what ifs" ("What if I make a mistake?" "What if I cause a penalty kick?" "What if I miss a penalty kick?" "What if we lose?"). Because a great deal of anxiety arises from fear of the unknown, focus on the things your child can control—for example, working hard, supporting teammates, and focusing on the positive.

Maintain a Sense of "Normalcy" Before a Match

Don't make game day into an enormous production, with "special" meals and rituals. Keep to a regular schedule; blend the upcoming competition into the family routine.

Become Aware of Your Own Anxieties

These have an enormous, though subtle, effect on your child. If you are tense before your child's game, imagine what kind of message you are sending! As a corollary, think honestly about why you are nervous before your child's soccer game. Aren't there more important things for you to worry about?

Keep Your Child from Obsessing about Pressure

The more a young athlete thinks about slipping up, the greater the chance he will. It becomes a self-fulfilling prophecy. Be alert to signs

Footnotes

The following letter from a young player to his parents ran in Maryland's *Montgomery Soccer, Inc. Newsletter.* Brief as it is, it speaks volumes about youth soccer.

Dear Mom and Dad,
I'm writing this letter because you've always told me to tell you if something bothered me. This has been on my mind a lot, but I can't get myself to talk about it.

Remember the other day when my team was playing? I hope you won't get mad, but you kind of embarrassed me. I missed a shot on goal because my opponent was right on me. I felt bad about that, but even worse when you yelled at the referee. Actually, the challenge was fair.

Later in the game, when the coach took me out so Josh could play, I felt bad that you got down on him, because he's trying to do a good job. He really loves soccer and coaching.

Dad, I know you want me to be a good player, and I really try as hard as I can. But I guess I can't measure up to what you want me to be. The way you act when I don't do good makes me feel like I've let you down. On the way home the other day, you didn't speak to me. You made me feel like I never want to play again.

I'm not very good, but I love to play and be with the other kids. But it seems the only time you're happy is when I do really good—even though you say sports is supposed to be fun and to learn. I want to have fun, but you keep taking it away. I didn't know you were going to get so upset because I'm not a star.

This is really hard, and that's why I have to write it to you. I used to be really happy when you came to my games. Some kids' parents never show up. But maybe it would be better if you stopped coming, so I wouldn't have to worry about disappointing you.

Love, Mike.

that your youngster is anxious about making a mistake and gently steer his thoughts in a more positive direction.

Help Your Child Relax

The more relaxed a child is, the greater the chance she will not succumb to pressure. Relaxation can take many forms—breathing exercises, visualizations—but the end result is the same: The less attention paid to performance, the less chance of making errors on the field. Help your child find the relaxation technique that works best for her.

EATING WELL

Eating well before a match can produce dramatic results. But we can't expect youngsters to automatically know what to eat, or when. They need guidance from parents—who may themselves not be sports nutritionists. Here are some pointers:

Nutritional Guidelines

High-Carbohydrate Foods Are More Easily Converted to Energy by the Body than Are Foods High in Protein Carbohydrates should comprise 55 to 65 percent of daily caloric intake, with only 10 to 15 percent coming from meat or protein-rich food (lean meat, poultry, seafood, dairy products, and beans). Eating too much protein and not enough carbohydrates denies muscles the energy they need to perform well. It is exercise—not extra protein—that builds muscle.

Which Foods Should You Encourage Your Young Athlete to Eat? Try breakfast cereals (though not high-fiber), oatmeal, bread, toast, rolls, bagels, pancakes (with as little butter or margarine as possible), cooked vegetables, pasta, rice, potatoes, fruit juice, and fresh, cooked, or dried fruit. Small servings of protein, such as lean chicken, fish, boiled or poached eggs, and low-fat yogurt, milk, and cottage cheese, are also recommended.

Meals Should Be Eaten Three to Four Hours before Game Time They should also be eaten in as relaxed and comfortable a setting as possible. If your child has only a short time before an upcoming game, consider a liquid meal such as soup; liquids are more easily digested than solids.

Certain Foods Should Be Left off the Menu before a Game These include hamburger, sausage, steak, fried chicken, doughnuts, French fries, rich sauces and dressings like mayonnaise, and high-fiber salads. Sweet or concentrated drinks and very salty or spicy foods can cause thirst and therefore should be avoided too.

Never Underestimate the Importance of Drinking Water Fluids, particularly water, should be taken thirty minutes prior to game time and consumed whenever possible during a match. Fluids regulate body temperature and prevent overheating. They also transport energy, vitamins, and minerals throughout the body by means of the circulatory system.

Good Nutrition Following Strenuous Activity Is Vital Poor nutrition following games and workouts can lead to chronic fatigue. Athletes can fail to "refuel" properly if they ingest too much protein, too many empty-carbohydrate snacks like cookies and potato chips, and too many greasy, fatty foods—or if they take in too few calories. An optimal "recovery diet" following a practice or match includes complex carbohydrate-rich foods, such as oats, buckwheat or whole-grain pancakes (eaten two to four hours after exercise, when muscles are most receptive to replacing their stores of glycogen fuel); wholesome fruits, vegetables, and juices, such as oranges and orange juice, bananas, raisins, dried apricots, potatoes, and winter squash (all containing potassium, lost through sweat); and of course, enough fluids to quench thirst—and then some.

BURNOUTS AND DROPOUTS

Burnout is a youth sports buzzword. Each year burnout affects younger and younger players—probably because of the even greater demands being placed on them. Today's young athletes are pressured to concentrate on a single sport at earlier ages than ever before. They play on competitive teams long before they reach their teens. The *travel* part of *travel teams* is taken quite literally, as boys and girls roam far and wide, playing tournaments weekend after weekend, month after month, year after year. And if it's not competition, it's training, on a variety of squads and in every venue imaginable. Between school, club, and ODP teams, plus soccer camps and other opportunities, it's a wonder players don't burn *up* as well as *out*.

Indications of Burnout

There are a number of ways to tell if your child is suffering burnout—or perhaps nearing it. One is that his get-up-and-go has got up and gone. A youngster who once looked forward to every training session, whose idea of a good time was heading down to the mall to check out the new stock at the soccer store, and who whiled away endless hours in class drawing soccer balls all over his notebook now can't wait until the end of the season. He seeks excuses not to practice, searches the sky for rain, even talks about playing lacrosse next season.

Rapport with his coach is fading fast. Where once his coach's every word was a commandment from on high, suddenly things aren't so rosy. A player who is burning out finds fault with practice sessions, game strategy, even his own lack of progress.

In addition, performance during games is uninspired (and that's being charitable). Other parents start to notice; they might even comment, "Boy, Jason sure isn't playing like he used to. It's like he's sleep-walking out there." Lethargy, distraction, and lack of creativity are all signs of burnout.

The First Step Toward Curing Burnout Is to Recognize It Exists

Scoffing "She's just going through a phase," fails dismally to address the issue. Unless you acknowledge there is a problem and work actively to address it, the problem will never be solved. A parent who suspects a child is burning out should ask probing questions: "If practice were called off today, would you be happy or sad?" "Is soccer still your favorite sport?"

Often a Change—Even a Small One—Helps

Parents should not allow a child to quit in the middle of a season—all youngsters need to learn the meaning of commitment—but that doesn't mean ruling out alternatives. How about your child playing a new position? Rather than your young goalkeeper giving up soccer altogether, suggest that he play out in the field. A longtime striker who feels unchallenged up front might renew her interest in the sport if she tries defense.

Another change involves a new team. Often the challenge of adapting to a new coach and new teammates provides the surge of adrenaline a burned-out player needs. If this proves impractical, a parent might arrange a workout with "new blood." A kick-around session with kids from a rival team may be just the thing to get the competitive juices flowing again.

There Is No Heresy in Suggesting a Sabbatical It's okay for a youngster to try lacrosse, or the piano or drama for that matter. Youngsters *should* experiment with different activities; how else can they discover the ones they truly love?

Soccer is such a superb game—such a wonderful vehicle for expressing creativity, intelligence, athletic skill, and competitiveness—that its attractiveness to players seldom disappears. Burnedout youngsters may just need a break from it. They may not always return to the same level of competition, but they nearly always retain a deep affection for what soccer represents and a strong appreciation for everything it takes to play. Eventually, they'll be back kicking.

Burnout Is Not Only for Your Child

The world of youth soccer is littered with the corpses of men and women who once were the workhorses of their children's teams and clubs. They volunteered for every committee, task force, project, and job they could. They coached, refereed, organized tournaments, led fund-raisers, lined fields, cooked for the concession stand, and stayed around to clean up afterward. They were the organizational equivalents of World Cup winners—yet, faster than you can say "FIFA," they were gone. They disappeared, victims of burnout.

Recognize Burnout Even Before Getting Involved While it may be hard to say no when asked to do a job, bailing out in the middle of it, or leaving soccer altogether, is worse.

The next time you are approached to volunteer, ask yourself:

> *Is the time commitment really what it seems, or will it end up being more?*
> *Am I the kind of person who turns every new task into a major project?*
> *How does this new commitment fit in with my other responsibilities?* Don't forget, these include family, work, and friends!
> *What do I think about the folks I'll be working with?* Will I enjoy spending umpteen hours, days, weeks, months, or years with them?
> *Am I interested in the task?* If you can't put your heart into it, don't even try.
> *Why are they asking me to do this?* Is it because I am supremely qualified, or because they can't get some other poor sucker to take it on?
> *Why am I even thinking of saying yes?* Is it because I can't say no—or I'm embarrassed to? Is it because I can't let anyone down? Is it because I'm the only one on earth who can be depended on to do anything right? Or is this honestly a task I've always yearned to do?

How Parents Can Avoid Their Own Burnout Now assuming you've volunteered after all, here are some ways to avoid burnout:

> *Find a supportive spouse.* In addition to emotional sustenance, a partner who understands your commitment to

soccer can screen phone calls, make meals, clean the house, and not complain when the kitchen table is hidden under an avalanche of rosters, passes, and permissions slips.

➤ *Raise independent children.* They can also make meals and clean the house as well as get themselves to practice on their own.

➤ *At the same time, avoid neglecting your kids.* Make sure you find time to talk with them—even if it's after you've roped them all into stuffing envelopes with you.

➤ *Work for an understanding boss.* Whether we're talking about your "real" job or your soccer one, it's important to have someone who understands that volunteerism is important to you.

➤ *Make use of your answering machine.* Let it monitor your calls. Respond immediately to those you must; return other calls at a more convenient time.

➤ *Switch focus.* It's easy to go postal if you spend every season looking at the same forms, dealing with the same issues, answering the same questions. But if you switch your focus every now and then, chances are you'll renew your vision for the task. Creative problem-solving makes things fun and refreshes the mind—and spirit.

➤ *Develop administrative skills.* These include typing and computer skills and the ability to delegate. The less you end up doing that's rote and routine, the less burned out you'll be.

➤ *Exercise at least three times a week.* Consider this an obligation, not a luxury!

➤ *Get away once in a while.* Whether you enjoy a bridge game, a walk on the beach, or classic car exhibitions, go for it—and don't let soccer interfere. If you happen to run into a fellow board member or coach during your free time, be polite. But whatever you do, don't get dragged into a conversation about youth soccer!

Dropout

A problem closely related to burnout—its bigger, badder cousin in fact—is dropout. Beginning in their midteens, large numbers of youngsters abandon soccer. And they are leaving at just the point when they should be reaping the physical, emotional, and social rewards for which the sport is justly famous.

A study conducted by the Youth Sports Institute at Michigan State University revealed a number of reasons why players between the ages of eleven and eighteen drop out. Among those cited: the desire to try other activities, work, the unavailability of teams, teams that are either too competitive or not competitive enough, the demands on time, friends quit, dislike of the coach, lack of playing time, injury, dislike of teammates, and waning interest. (Though not mentioned specifically in the survey, dating is another reason teenagers stop playing soccer!)

Parents are often upset when their children quit soccer—especially when those parents have invested untold hours and dollars into the game. However, they should recognize that the desire to try other activities, for example, is quite legitimate. It is up to parents to send the message that experimenting with a new activity does not necessarily mean giving up soccer forever.

While most teenagers today have jobs—and that's good; work enables them to earn money, develop self-confidence, and learn about "the real world"—too many adolescents work too many hours at the expense of recreation. Parents should keep an eye on their children's work schedule, especially if it cuts deeply into their free time.

Many of the other reasons youngsters quit can be addressed by concerned parents. For example, if the coach has an attitude not conducive to continuing play, parents can help youngsters form a new team or find one that works.

Finally, every youngster who quits does not have to be lured back to soccer. There is a time to play and a time to rest. If a young player clearly has had it with the game, mothers and fathers need to accept that. After all, youth soccer is just that: *youth* soccer. It is not *parent* soccer.

CHAPTER 5
Equipment

Helping your child choose the proper equipment is important and contributes to his or her enjoyment of soccer.

IF THE SHOE FITS

"If the shoe fits, wear it," may have been good advice once upon a time—but in the world of soccer today, it doesn't have a leg to stand on.

An explosion of technology, design, and fashion have turned buying soccer shoes into a formidable task. Players today—and parents who foot (so to speak) the bill—face a dizzying array of choices.

At the same time, shoes, boots, cleats—whatever you call them, those things that get laced up just before a youngster takes to the field—are the most important part of the soccer player's uniform. Let's face it, a sharp-looking jersey has never won a soccer match. But plenty of games have been lost due to improper footwear.

Choosing the Right Footwear

What does a parent need to know about the heart and "sole" of soccer shoes?

Footwear Is Important for Two Reasons First, soccer is a running game (up to nine miles a game!), and an athlete runs best when he feels comfortable. Second, soccer is the only game that highlights the lower extremities; the feet are used to impart direction, speed, and spin to the ball. A player who cannot *feel* the ball because of ill-fitting shoes will never be able to play to his full potential.

Shoes Serve Three Primary Functions: Traction, Flexibility, and Support Traction is achieved through the pattern, height, and size of the cleats. (Technically, *cleats* refers to the studs, not to the entire shoe.) Shoes should be flexible only where the foot is flexible; otherwise pain and even injury may result. Support is important because soccer players constantly plant their feet and change direction. The shoe should allow the heel to lock and prevent the forefoot from rolling excessively. An unsupported foot invites injury.

The Best Value Can Be Determined by Comparing Features of Different Shoes in a Particular Price Range Features include type of leather, whether a sole is removable or not, and the form of the heel cup. But don't underestimate the importance of looks. No youngster wants to wear anything that is out of fashion, and that includes soccer shoes. Though color and style should not be determining factors, they do mean a lot to young soccer players.

The Player Is the One Who Selects the Shoes She will be the one wearing them. Encourage her to try on many pairs, wearing the kind and number of socks she will wear during a match. Have her plant her foot; check to see that the shoe is wide enough to spread when a player's entire weight is placed on it. When she stands up straight, her toes should be snug against the shoe. She should also try juggling a soccer ball with the shoes on to ensure their comfort (any store that will not allow this should not be selling soccer equipment!).

Avoid Purchasing Shoes that Are Too Big Players will never grow into such shoes; they will have quit long before. Oversized shoes can cause injuries including stubbed toes and turned ankles. They also retard proper development by throwing off coordination and diminishing the *feel* the player has for the ball. They even invite teasing: "Hey, Sasquatch!"

Avoid Purchasing Shoes That Are Too Small An old saying advised: The smaller the shoe, the better the player. But shoes today do not stretch as they once did, so forget about size-ten athletes buying size-eight shoes. If a shoe fits comfortably, buy it.

Beginners Should Buy Sturdy Shoes New players need solid instep and toe protection, because they are more apt to suffer minor injuries and bruises due to poor kicking and trapping technique. And they should play only in shoes with flat or molded soles—no screw-in cleats! Beginners need support and feel more than they do added traction and any "intimidation factor."

Be Sure to Look for Certain Features The upper part of the shoe should be made of quality leather that is soft and preferably full grain. (A synthetic fiber is fine for younger children, who outgrow shoes quickly.) Good lateral support helps prevent ankle and knee injuries.

The shoe should be reinforced from midheel forward to the arch and from around the toe backward to the arch. Good arch support helps ward off shin splints. The heel should be rounded and narrow enough to fit snugly. The toe should be reinforced, with the toe box wide enough for comfort.

On Wet or Muddy Fields or in Thick, High Grass, Use Screw-in Cleats
These sturdy studs allow for excellent traction. Mud does not accumulate as easily between screw-in cleats, and the length of individual studs can be varied depending on the precise conditions of the field. Players shouldn't be able to feel the studs when they're wearing them, however. If they do, they should switch to shoes with a molded sole. And screw-ins should never be worn on dry, resistant surfaces, or players risk not only blisters but also serious wear and tear on joints and ligaments.

On Dry or Well-Mowed Fields Wear* Molded-Sole *Shoes These bottoms are softer and more flexible than screw-ins; they do not penetrate the ground, but since nothing does on a hard surface anyway, *moldeds* end up providing better traction. They feature more studs than do screw-ins; by spreading the player's weight over a larger number of cleats, they reduce the chance of discomfort as well as of blisters and injuries when playing on resistant surfaces.

Special Shoes Are Available for Artificial Turf Molded shoes work well on artificial turf; once in decline, they now feature improved polyurethane and rubber. However, those who play many games a year on artificial surfaces often prefer specially designed turf shoes with numerous rubber minicleats that penetrate the turf's small fibers. For playing once or twice a season, though, indoor soccer shoes (see below) or even sneakers are fine.

Soccer Flats *Are Great for Indoors* These flat-soled shoes are similar to basketball sneakers in terms of traction. However, because they are also used for kicking, they are lighter and more durable.

Shoes Should Be Broken in Slowly They should not be worn in a match the same day they were bought—unless the player wants to grow a garden of blisters. New shoes should be soaked in lukewarm water, then dried on the feet while the player walks around. As the shoes dry, they conform to the contours of the foot. New shoes should be worn in practice prior to a game for the sake of familiarity and also to prevent poor performance due to uncomfortable shoes.

Soccer Shoes Should Not Be Cleaned in a Washing Machine Instead, mud and dirt can be removed manually with mild soap and cold water. The shoes should then be air dried away from any direct heat source, such as a radiator. Once shoes are dry, leather conditioner, polish, or saddle soap helps replace the leather's natural oils. Shoes should be polished often, in wet and dry weather. A shoe tree or stuffing of newspaper can help them retain their shape. Parents may be amazed to see youngsters lavishing more care and attention on soccer shoes than on any other article of clothing—but then again, a child may value his soccer shoes over anything else he wears.

Do Not Lace Shoes Too Tightly Constricting the instep prevents players from feeling the ball. Shoes should instead be laced snuggly but comfortably, straight across, with the laces tucked on the outside of the shoe. Most coaches frown upon tying the laces up around the sock. Shorter, rather than longer, laces lessen the chance an opponent's spike will get caught in one.

You Can Avoid the High Cost of Soccer Shoes Try buying from neighbors or from thrift or consignment shops; alternatively, clubs can organize "shoe swaps." However, parents should never skimp on buying good shoes. Their child's comfort—and safety—are at stake.

SENDING YOUR CHILD OFF TO WAR— ER, GAMES: THE EQUIPMENT BAG

An equipment bag is as important to a young soccer player as a backpack is to a student. It's amazing the amount of "stuff" that can be stuffed into such a bag (and amazing, too, what happens when it is not aired out frequently enough).

Other Equipment

What does a youth soccer player truly need?

Uniform Jersey, shorts, socks, and shoes are key. Players who don't wear their uniforms to a match should pack them the night before; that way they're sure to have them. For all players, it's a good idea to bring the alternate jersey (in the event of a color conflict). You can never go wrong with an extra pair of shoes either.

Shin Guards Most leagues and tournaments will not let a player on the field without this vital piece of equipment. It never hurts to carry an extra pair (see above).

Ball Be sure the player's name is on it—in permanent ink.

Pump Ball pump.

Stud Wrench For players who wear screw-in cleats. (And, of course, extra cleats.)

Warmups Light or heavy, depending on the weather.

Athletic Tape This serves a variety of purposes beyond supporting ankles, from holding up socks to mending shoes and keeping on bandages. Your child will go through athletic tape the same way he goes through food after a game, so be sure to keep plenty on hand.

Beverages and Snacks Nonperishable, such as fruit, water, and boxes of fruit juice.

Sunscreen Your child may not like to hear your constant reminders about it, but preventing sunburn at an early age is crucial to preventing skin cancer in later years.

SHOOT! (THE CAMERA, THAT IS)

Tired of pacing, yelling, and biting your fingernails on the sidelines? How about becoming a photographer or videographer? Finally, you can put all that equipment you bought years ago to good use.

Camera Tips
If you're into cameras or camcorders, keep the following in mind:

A Good 35-mm Camera Is Better than a Range Finder Beginners should use a zoom telephoto lens with variable focus lengths (though lenses with a fixed focal length are easier to handle and may deliver better picture quality). If you don't have a telephoto, be patient, and wait until the subject comes close enough to shoot.

Aim Your Shots Depending on the Width of Your Lens When using anything less than a 135-mm lens, stick with goalmouth or sideline shots directly in front of you. If you've got a 200-mm lens, you can expand your shots to the penalty box or into the field. A 300-mm lens enables you to reach the midfield.

Don't Shoot into the Light Though autofocus is wonderful for most photography, it's not always good for soccer action. It's just not quick enough to capture the game's fast pace.

Use Film with the Lowest ASA Rating Possible Except for very cloudy days, 100 ASA film is usually sufficient.

Become Familiar with the Game Only then can you anticipate who will be where, and when, and what will happen next.

Success Comes Only through Practice As with your child on the field, the more you're out there taking shots, the better your anticipation, timing, and reflexes will be.

Look Off the Field for Shots Sideline reactions, excited fans, delirious or dejected players, even stray dogs, all make for wonderful photos.

Be Patient Just like a soccer goal, good photographs seldom come easily. But if you work hard enough, they will happen.

Watch Out for the Linesman He has every right to run up and down the sideline without knocking into a camera-wielding spectator. And be prepared to move away from the goal if an official asks you to. This is a reasonable request, made in consideration of players' safety—and your own.

With Camcorder in Hand, Figure Out the Purpose of Your Video If it is to record the entire game for analysis by players and coaches, choose a high elevation in the center of the field. A tripod is a must. Shoot at an angle wide enough to catch action as it develops away from the ball.

If, on the other hand, you simply want to show off your child for friends, relatives, and posterity, this high, midfield angle becomes boring after a while, so use it sparingly. You can shoot close-ups better from ground level. If your child is a striker, shoot (the camera, that is) from behind the net. Pick up the dribbler, follow the action, and widen your view to include the whole goal area when it appears a shot will be attempted. If your child is a goalkeeper, also shoot from behind the net (though you'll only get the back view). And avoid the temptation to focus solely on your child. You love her, sure—but she's got ten teammates on the field, and eleven opponents. Include them in the action too.

Stick to the Basics Avoid "artsy" shots and too-frequent cuts between wide-angle views and close-ups. You're trying to film a soccer match, not win an Academy Award—or induce vertigo in your viewers. The less you move your camera, the better off everyone will be. Panning (moving the camera horizontally) should be done only for a purpose, such as following the action or showing a panoramic view. And panning should always be done s-l-o-w-l-y! If you must walk during shooting (done properly, an effective technique), be sure your lens is at its widest focal length. Take small steps, bend your knees, and *concentrate*. As for zooming, it's usually most effective to stop the camera, zoom to something, then restart.

Shoot with Your Back to the Sun Be aware of backgrounds too. For best results, they should be darker than your subject.

Stop Shooting during Dead Time No one is interested in watching players chase balls into the woods or coaches jog onto the field following an injury. If you film the action and only the action, everyone will want to watch; if the game is as long on tape as it was on the field, no one will.

Maintain a Steady Hand Practice holding the camera still. Try holding your breath and locking your elbows into your ribs. Better yet, invest in a tripod.

Don't Forget Halftime It's a great opportunity to capture players who might not be in the game much as well as to shoot (figuratively, of course) some of the sideline characters.

Silence Is Golden Though the sounds of kicks, whistles, and on-field communication are of interest, they're sometimes drowned out by thoughtless comments made by nearby spectators or (perish the thought) the cameraperson himself or herself. To avoid undue embarrassment, stifle the audio.

CHAPTER 6
Helpful Hints

S occer is all about communication. Players talk constantly on the field: They warn each other of open men, encourage teammates to shoot, and call for the ball. Coaches communicate with players: They instruct them during training sessions, call out helpful hints during games, and console and encourage them when they're down. Parents must communicate with each other too; otherwise armies of minivans would wander lost down our freeways, and who would know whose turn it was to slice oranges?

TALKING TO THE COACH

But one of the most important forms of communication takes place between parents and the coach. This type of talk plays a crucial role in determining the success or failure of a child's experience with youth soccer. A well-meaning yet overly aggressive parent can torpedo his daughter's relationship with her coach, just as a timid parent who never says boo can miss out on a chance to help her son improve his game.

When communicating with your child's coach, bear in mind:

Less Is Best

Coaches are busy people, and they're volunteering their time. They don't have time to listen to every comment, complaint, or question that pops into a parent's head. Ideally, the majority of their time is spent communicating with boys and girls, not moms and dads. (And parents should encourage children to learn to talk to the coach; it's one of those life lessons that soccer is so good at teaching.) Obviously, there are times when a parent should—indeed, *must*—consult with the coach. But these should be kept to a minimum.

Pick a Good Time to Talk

Determine when the coach has free time, and is unlikely to be distracted. Now for some inopportune times to initiate a discussion:

- ➤ In the middle of practice.
- ➤ Right before a game. Right after a game.
- ➤ Halftime.
- ➤ Six in the morning.
- ➤ Midnight.
- ➤ Holidays

Keep Personalities Out of It

Focus on the issues at hand. Don't get sidetracked by talking about how the coach treated your older son on last winter's basketball team, or what his daughter did to your daughter on the playground two years ago. If you have other issues with the coach, fine—but don't air them in a soccer forum.

Footnotes

A Massachusetts U-14 girls coach filed assault charges against the parent of one of his players after the father grabbed him by the throat, dragged him across the floor, and threatened to kill him for not giving the man's daughter more playing time in an indoor match. "It's crazy," the coach said. "If he'd wanted to sit down and discuss it with me, I'd have been more than happy to."

Stick to Facts, Not Rumors

If you did not see it with your own eyes, don't mention it. Your child may be upset that she played "like five minutes" in one game when in fact it was fifteen. Or perhaps you've heard that the coach "screamed" at the team at halftime, when in fact he merely expressed his disappointment at their play. Most important, steer clear of anything you hear from other parents. Sideline chatter should be treated as gossip, not gospel.

Communicate Minor Concerns Before They Become Major Ones

It does no one any good to let a problem fester. If you have an issue you truly believe is important, bring it up with the coach sooner rather than later.

Ask, Don't Demand

No one wants to start out a conversation on the defensive. Instead of demanding, "Why hasn't Lissa started the last two games? You started her in the beginning of the year!" try opening with "I was wondering why you've decided to change the lineup recently. Has Lissa been slacking off in games or practices? Or is there some other reason? Can I do something to help her improve?" Giving a coach—anyone, really—a chance to explain himself at the beginning goes a long way to ensuring that the encounter does not degenerate into shouts or threats.

Listen, Don't Interrupt

Asking a question implies that you want an answer. Hear the coach out. Consider her response. Frame a reply. If you do not care to hear the coach's side of a story, don't request it.

Volunteer Your Skills and Experience

If you've got a playing or coaching background, by all means, offer to assist the coach. But don't go further than offering. No telling the coach how to run practice sessions, which player to place where, and what kind of formation to use. If you lack the time or inclination to coach yourself, and the current coach doesn't appear to appreciate your input, then you have no choice but to keep your opinions to yourself.

If the coach is a friend, neighbor, colleague, or relative, don't talk soccer at all. There is no quicker way to ruin a friendship or other close relationship.

REFEREES

Referees are the bane of every—well, many—parents of youth soccer players. Moms and dads have a difficult time seeing how anyone could ever call a foul on their child—or, conversely, how anyone could *not* red-card the entire opposing team for their rough, unsportsmanlike, in fact astonishingly *evil,* play.

But let's face it: Without referees, the game of soccer could not exist. The men, women, and children in black (and, nowadays, purple and other colors) have an exceptionally difficult task. They must enforce the rules while allowing the match to proceed without undue interruption. They must prevent injuries, yet allow certain types of contact to occur. They must reinforce for youngsters the rules of the game as well as its spirit. And they must do all that in spite of constant criticism from players, coaches, and spectators.

A referee, it is said, is someone who must be perfect from day one, and then get better each match.

Some "Official" Hints

The next time you are tempted to gnash your teeth, scream "!@#$%&*", or commit the ultimate foul (murder), keep these thoughts in mind:

Officials Do Not Make Bad Calls on Purpose They are not out to get your team or make sure the other team wins. They are human beings, and human beings occasionally make mistakes.

Soccer Needs Referees Too many officials quit each year, often because of too much abuse and too little support. Each referee who leaves must be replaced—and each replacement, naturally, is less experienced than the one who left.

Refereeing Is Not as Easy as it Looks Whistling a match from the middle is far more difficult than doing it from the sidelines. There are constant and continual judgment calls, shades of gray, moments of indecision. Officiating demands fitness, stamina, levelheadedness, an

Footnotes

The referee's decision was controversial: A twelve-year-old boy could not play in the finals of a Massachusetts tournament because he would not remove his bandanna. The boy had a good reason: He was a Sikh, the follower of a religion that requires adherents to cover their heads in public. And he had worn the bandanna without incident all season long, including four previous tournament games.

Still, the referee was insistent. He cited tourney rules against bandannas. He said it was "a safety issue, cut and dried. Someone could grab the bandanna and yank his head back."

Coaches and parents from both teams pleaded the boy's case; the opposing coach, in fact, noted that the bandanna had "no bearing whatsoever" on the game. But tournament officials adamantly upheld the rule.

The boy's teammates refused to play. So did their opponents. Nevertheless, tournament officials declared the opposing team the winner. When they received their first-place trophies, players presented one to the boy at the center of the controversy.

"It was an absolute miracle," his mother said. "It was a blessing to our religion and family to see how the teams responded." The youngster added, "I was really mad—that's the first thing that came to mind. But when everyone supported me, I felt a lot better."

As a final bit of good news, parents from both teams organized a posttournament cookout and pickup game. "It's not about settling the score," said the coach of the boy's team. "It's about showing appreciation."

extraordinary command of the rules, a healthy dose of psychology, and a thick skin.

Remember the Old Saying: "If You Can't Say Anything Nice . . ."
When a game is over, it's unrealistic to expect an official to change a call; all decisions, right or wrong, have already been made, and nothing can alter the outcome. Venting your spleen will not solve anything; what it will do is upset the official and make you look like a fool. Persistent problems with an official should be settled by the coach or team manager.

On the Other Hand, if You Can Say Something Nice, Do It! Because referees are indeed human, they appreciate praise as much as the rest of us. This is especially important in the case of young officials. Remember: Every young official is someone else's daughter or son.

The Game Is for the Players No matter how frustrated you may be, creating problems for officials takes the match away from the athletes.

Referees Make Fewer Mistakes in a Game than Any Single Player
Players—even those at the World Cup level—often misdirect their kicks, fail to control passes, and err in their choices on the field. Refs do exhibit poor judgment—but nowhere near as often as players.

Referees Do Not Win or Lose Matches The game of soccer is actually won (and lost) on the training field. Let's say your child's team loses a game because of "that lousy penalty-kick call." Does that mean the team had no other chance to score? Come to think of it, why was the ball bouncing around in their penalty area anyway? Sounds like your youngster's team should spend more time practicing their shooting and their defense, and their parents less time placing blame where it does not belong!

ON THE ROAD AGAIN

Willie Nelson's ode to the travelin' life no doubt resonates with many youth soccer parents. Endlessly shuttling back and forth between try-outs, practices, games, tournaments, camps, and pizza parties, a mom or dad can spend what seems like several lifetimes in the driver's seat of that official vehicle of youth soccer, the minivan.

Regarding those interminable hours when the only thing you're lacking to be a full-fledged chauffeur is the uniform, this valuable advice bears repeating. Play dumb. Do, however, keep your ears wide open. You'll be amazed at the information you pick up.

Now let's talk about that staple of youth soccer: tournament travel. Sometimes parents are called upon to chaperone youth soccer teams during out-of-town, out-of-state, even overseas soccer tournaments. Such trips may result in numerous adventures whose humor may not be appreciated until years later in the retelling; these usually involve van and airplane rides, hotel rooms, and the less-than-mature ways young soccer players view the world and everyone in it. However, with a little foresight, such incidents need not involve tournament officials, hoteliers, or law enforcement agents.

Chaperone Tips

If, as one of your many volunteering jobs in youth soccer, you ever turn into a tournament chaperone, you'll do yourself a big favor to read what follows.

Chaperones Must Be Prepared for "Testing" in a New Environment
They should formulate standards of conduct (ideally, with the help of
the players), and they should communicate those standards early and
often. They should know how they will handle various transgressions:
breaking curfew, missing a team meeting, tormenting a teammate.
Everyone should be aware of the consequences if a rule is broken.
And chaperones must be prepared to follow through.

Chaperones and Coaches Should Agree on the Exercise of Authority
Who will make disciplinary decisions? What form of appeal will a mis-
creant have? And what constitutes the final court of appeal?

Encourage Players to Interact with the People They Meet These
include other players, referees, coaches, even random people on the
street. Soccer can open a door to the wider world—a door youngsters
sometimes need to be nudged through. If they hang out with the
same friends every time they travel, they will never take full advantage
of all that the experience of travel offers. They may not realize it at the
time—but a few years down the road they'll certainly appreciate your
gentle prodding.

*If You're Traveling Overseas, Make Sure Players Have at Least a
Rudimentary Knowledge of Geography, Currency, Language,
Habits, and Customs of Host Countries* True, English is becoming
the world's lingua franca, and America's ignorance of the rest of the
planet is common knowledge. But your players are under no obligation to perpetuate the stereotype of the American who thinks the
world revolves around him. Players who exhibit even the tiniest little bit of knowledge about their hosts find that it takes them a very
long way.

Be Alert for Homesickness This can strike youngsters (and old-sters!) of any age, but it's more apt to hit children as well as play-ers who have rarely been away from home, who are missing a fam-ily event like a birthday or wedding, or who were in the midst of some emotional upheaval when they left. Signs of homesickness include isolation from the group, a constant need to call home, a change in behavioral patterns (such as eating habits or playing style), and an inordinate desire to be with adults. Often simply pay-ing a little extra attention to a homesick youngster, offering a sym-pathetic ear, and making a special effort to include him in activities, will help.

Keep a Close Watch on Players Who Squander Money There's at least one on every team. They make big (often seemingly senseless) pur-chases. They ask to borrow money, promising to pay it back later. Be prepared to confiscate their money for safekeeping and to put them on a daily allowance.

Locate a Laundromat Make sure you have plenty of change and detergent with you. Also bring along safety pins so players can attach their shorts and socks to their jerseys for easy identification.

Pack Snacks That Carry Easily, Will Not Spoil, and Are High in Carbohydrates Healthful snacks include energy bars, bagels, bran muffins, banana bread, whole-grain breads, and string cheese, pret-zels, rice cakes, wheat crackers, apples, fig bars, oatmeal raisin cookies, granola bars, raisins, dried fruit and juice boxes, and snack-size tuna. Nutritious snacks sold at the airport include soft pretzels, salads, sand-wiches, and fruit bowls.

Stock Up on Food at Grocery Stores, Not Convenience Markets Groceries offer salad bars, bakeries for bagels and fresh bread, individual yogurt cups, and fresh fruits and vegetables. At the grocery store salad bar, encourage athletes to mix different types of lettuce, spinach, and cabbage and top with fresh vegetables; go easy on shredded cheese and crumbled eggs, and avoid croutons, bacon bits, and mayonnaise-based salads.

When the Team Heads to a Restaurant, Steer Them Toward Italian Recommended dishes include pasta with marinara sauce, pizza (plain or with vegetables), and salads (with dressing on the side).

At Meals Split Several Small Groups Five tables of four can be seated and served in half the time a gang of twenty can be accommodated. Choose your dining spot carefully, based on the age, number, and maturity of your players.

Sometimes a Fast-Food Restaurant Is Unavoidable In that case, players should avoid milk shakes, sausage and egg croissants, sausage biscuits, cherry turnovers, danishes, scrambled eggs, bacon double deluxe cheeseburgers (and all their relatives), hot dogs (especially with chili or cheese), chicken nuggets, and of course french fries, along with such seemingly healthful items as salad dressings and toppings (cheese sauces, sour cream, mayonnaise, bacon, ketchup, and tartar sauce), which are actually high in fat. For breakfast, urge athletes to order toast, bagels, whole-grain cereals and breads. For other meals charbroiled or roasted sandwiches (especially chicken) get thumbs-up, as do plain baked potatoes, salad bars, juice, low-fat milk, and cheese or vegetable pizza with a thin or hand-tossed crust.

APPENDIX A
The Camp Experience

S occer camp has become as much a part of summer as water slides, bug zappers and action-packed, earth-destroying movies. Each summer, tens of thousands of youngsters run (actually, most are driven) to soccer camp. Many have a great time there; they improve, make new friends, and grow physically and emotionally. Some have a less rewarding experience. Whatever the outcome, soccer camp belongs to youth players, not their mothers and fathers. However, parents can do their part to make sure the camp experience is as good as it can be.

CHOICES, CHOICES

Be prepared to choose from a wide variety of camps, including day (full and half day), overnight, and those that include both day campers and boarders. There are camps that run for one week and those that extend for as long as three. There are camps in a family's backyard, and those so far away that players need a passport (literally) to get there. There are coed camps and camps just for boys, or just for girls. Some camps handle a wide age range, while others are limited to, say, seven- to nine-year-olds. Some are run by local clubs or associations, others by high school or college coaches, still others that are unaffiliated. Certain camps specify "for elite players" or "advanced" only. A relatively new innovation is camps that train entire teams together. And there are "soccer-only" camps as well as those that offer plenty of soccer instruction but also include activities like swimming and even camping.

Here's a look at some advantages and disadvantages of certain kinds of camps.

> *Day camps.* They're easy to get to, cost less than overnight camps, and are less intense (which can be good or bad). Day camps that are run by local clubs provide coaching that is consistent with the club and its philosophies; however, they offer less exposure to different coaching styles, have less continuity from year to year, and usually are held at facilities that are not as nice as those at boarding schools or colleges.

> *Soccer-only camps.* A child can concentrate on the sport he loves. He will be surrounded by like-minded campers and staffers. He will definitely improve by handling a soccer ball several hours a day, several days in a row. If he can

handle that intensity, great. However, some children get bored or distracted easily; others are just too young to handle soccer twenty-four hours a day, seven days a week. Nothing can kill a love for the game faster than overkill.

➤ *"Specialty" camps.* Some camps specialize in goalkeepers. There are also "striker" camps that concentrate on shooting (as yet there are none specializing in midfield play or defense). The best ones are superb. There are more specialized drills, workouts, and concepts than any ordinary human being can fathom. The people who run these camps imbue youngsters with an understanding of one position that is, for better or worse, manic. Be forewarned: These camps are not for the faint of heart. It is difficult to ask a child to play one position hour after hour, then sit down and takes notes on abstract theories.

QUESTIONS TO ASK

It is a parent's job to make sense out of this broad range of camps. You can start by asking why you should send your child to soccer camp in the first place. Does she have a passion for the game and seem to be unable to live without her soccer ball? Or does she just want to keep up with her friends?

Is your child the independent sort, or has she never been away from home? Are any friends going—and if not, does that matter to her? Has she been exposed to different coaches, or will this be a new experience?

Does your child enjoy playing soccer with the opposite gender (or perhaps enjoy it a bit too much)?

Once you and your child have decided that soccer camp is a good idea, start narrowing down the options. Seek recommendations from coaches and from parents whose children have already gone. Scour *Soccer America*, *Soccer Jr.*, and regional and local soccer newspapers for camp ads (most print special "camp issues," usually in late winter or early spring).

If a camp is run by a big-name college coach or professional player, inquire whether he or she will actually be there—and for how long. Some "stars" may appear for one day only and even then do no actual instruction; others are always on site, offering a true hands- (and feet)-on approach. Some college coaches are really only organizers; they run many different camps each summer and may never show up at all. Other coaches are intimately involved with every detail. Find out exactly what the situation is. (A good way to begin is by asking to speak to the "name"—and seeing how far you get.)

You should also ask how many hours a day are spent on soccer activities and how that time is divided between instruction, practice, and games. If the camp is coed, determine how skills groups are created and whether teams are mixed or separated for games.

Ask about the staff. Where do the instructors hail from? (Remember that foreign accents, while interesting, are no measure of reliability or good instruction). What are their ages? What are their coaching—as opposed to playing—credentials? (A great player is not necessarily a great, or even adequate, coach.) How many have been affiliated with the camp before and for how long? What is the ratio of camper to staff (and how many are instructors as opposed to counselors)? Who is in charge of supervision: the instructors or other staff members? What is the overall philosophy of the camp?

What is the daily schedule? How much rest do campers get? How much time is spent on the following: fundamentals, strategy and tactics, small-sided games, full-field games, videos and lectures, evening activities?

Inquire, too, about medical attention: Is there a doctor on staff or at least on call nearby? What about a trainer?

Facilities are important as well. In particular: How many fields are there (and how many campers are there per field)? How far are they from everything else? Is there access to indoor facilities in the case of inclement weather? Go ahead and ask about the sleeping accommodations (how many campers to a room and whether or not the rooms are air-conditioned), but avoid making this your primary consideration.

Ask whether there is a camp store, and if so, what it sells and for how much. Some camps make huge profits off the sale of everything from balls, jerseys, shorts, and socks to junk food and soda. Others simply sell necessities at bargain prices.

As for scholarships or financial aid, not all camps offer them. But it never hurts to ask.

GETTING READY

Once you have decided on a camp, it's time to get ready.

Any soccer camp, no matter how low-key, is a physically challenging experience. Youngsters train for several hours a day; there may even be games at night, followed by instructional videos or other activities. The ability to pay attention decreases with fatigue, and the ability to train is hindered if a child suffers from aches and pains, even if they are minor. Do not send your child off to camp in "couch potato" shape.

Most camps provide packing lists; adhere to them closely. Of particular importance: plenty of jerseys, shorts, underwear, and socks (more than you imagine—youngsters may change several times a day, and laundry facilities might be primitive); more towels than you'd expect; soccer shoes that are already broken in (new shoes are a certain recipe for blisters); petroleum jelly (because blisters inevitably pop up, old shoes or new); indoor shoes for evening and bad-weather play; rain gear; shower sandals; a small electric fan (if the dorms lack air-conditioning); alarm clock; calling card or change for telephone calls; water bottle; bug spray; sunscreen; adhesive bandages; spending money. Check carefully to see if your child needs to bring a ball, if one is provided, or if he can purchase one there (and what it will cost).

One final note: Even if the packing list says nothing about extra food, send along some snacks. No matter how good the cooks are, young soccer players always benefit from a stash of healthful grub (such as dried fruit) and beverages (including powdered drinks to mix with water; don't forget a plastic bottle). Good snacks are also a great way to help your youngster make new friends.

THE CALL HOME

If (that is, when) your child calls, be positive. He might complain about anything: The food is horrible, the rooms are too small, the coach has him playing a new position; the drills are too easy; the drills are too hard; the players are too weak or too strong.

Whether or not these complaints are valid is beside the point. You, as a parent, cannot do anything about them—nor should you. Part of the experience of soccer camp is learning how to be an athlete, and being an athlete means adapting to and overcoming adverse conditions. Don't worry about any short-term annoyances. If the camp is a good one—and most are—the long-term benefits will prevail.

APPENDIX B
Selecting a College

College: for many youth soccer players, the Holy Grail. Visions of full scholarships, exotic travel, and national championships dance through youngsters' (and, of course, their parents') heads. In fact, the need to gain an advantage in the great college quest is often cited as a reason for the proliferation of highly competitive teams of young players.

In reality, soccer is nothing like football and basketball—at least when it comes to college athletics. The number of available soccer scholarships pales in comparison; the amount of money awarded is even less. At most universities today, soccer remains a second-tier sport.

For all but a few elite players, the recruiting process works backward: Rather than coaches luring athletes to a college or university, high school soccer players must convince a coach they will benefit that coach's program. The burden—at least at the beginning—is on the player, not the coach. The role of parents in the process is limited. Coaches are looking at how independent a player is, and a hovering parent turns them off.

College coaches are also turned off by an unending parade of letters, phone calls, faxes, and E-mails about young prodigies. Such aggressive lobbying often backfires.

As one National College Athletics Association coach remarks, "I'm seeing a large percentage of initial letters come not from the athlete, but from the mother or father. It's very obvious when a résumé is put together by the parents and run off on the color copier at the office. I get a sixty-page packet on a kid, and I know the same thing was sent to fifty-two other schools. Or I pick up the phone and a secretary says, 'Please hold for Mr. Jones.' Well, I've never spoken to Mr. Jones before, and here he is calling about his son."

When a player contacts a coach directly, the coach can assume the player's motivation is there. However, when a parent makes the contact, the coach cannot be sure. Plus, a player who avoids making the initial contact herself may not be emotionally ready for the transition from high school to college. It does not bode well for an eighteen-year-old about to go off on her own if she can't even pick up a telephone.

College soccer is not a continuation of the youth soccer experience. Instead, beginning with recruiting, it marks a time for athletes to separate from parents. It initiates a growth period during which players make their own decisions about programs and priorities. And under no condition should parents contact coaches once the player is on the team to inquire about playing time, positioning, or any other soccer-related matter. As one college coach pointedly asks, "When their kid graduates, gets his first job, and has his first problem at work, what are they going to do? Call the boss and complain?"

Now here are some ways parents can help.

PLANNING

Spring of your child's junior year is a good time to begin planning for college. Coaches are done recruiting for the season and can answer letters thoroughly and thoughtfully. You and your child can also visit campuses without bumping into the masses of high schoolers who descend every fall. Resources you can help provide include individual college catalogs and CD-ROMs as well as general college guides. Books and magazines dedicated to college athletics include the following:

➤ *Official Athletic College Guide to Soccer.* Published annually and edited by Charlie Kadupski. Contact: The Sport Source, 2701-C W. 15th St., Suite 162, TX 75075; 1-800-862-3092.

➤ *The Soccer America College Guide.* Published each spring by *Soccer America* magazine. Contact: Soccer America, P.O. Box 23704, Oakland, CA 94623; (510) 528-5000.

➤ *NCAA Guide for the College-Bound Student Athlete.* A pamphlet with general information about Divisions I, II, and III. Contact: NCAA, 6201 College Blvd., Overland Park, KS 66211; (913) 339-1906.

➤ *National Directory of College Athletics.* Includes addresses, phones, and fax numbers for NCAA, NAIA, NJCAAA, NCCAA, and CCCAA coaches (and deciphers all those acronyms for you too). Contact: Collegiate Directories, P.O. Box 450640, Cleveland, OH 44145; (216) 835-1172.

➤ *Advising Student Athletes Through the College Recruitment Process.* A book by Michael Koehler. Includes samples of letters, memos, and other materials to use when communicating with coaches. Contact: Prentice Hall, Englewood Cliffs, NJ 07632.

> ➤ *The Ultimate Recruitment Guide and Notebook.* A 250-page guide by David Kaplan for potential student-athletes. Offers sections on personal experiences and advice from the pros. Contact: The Integrity Group, 20546 N. Milwaukee Ave., Suite 555, Deerfield, IL 60015; 1-800-436-6468.

BEING REALISTIC

Avoid encouraging your child to apply to a school that is far beyond his reach, either on the field or in the classroom. And don't apply pressure on your child to receive a soccer scholarship; again, they're nearly as rare as hat tricks in the World Cup. Honest discussion about money is in order. High school students need to know what their families can and cannot afford—not so players feel obligated to win scholarships but so they can focus their college search realistically.

ASKING THE RIGHT QUESTIONS

Help your son or daughter frame reflective questions: How important is college soccer to me? Will I be happy at a Division III college, or do I need the hustle and bustle of a Division I university? Am I willing to work for a couple of years until I earn a varsity spot? How important is location (area of country, urban/suburban/rural, etc.)?

Next suggest topics to raise with a college coach: Where is the soccer program headed in the next couple of years—will it become more competitive or less? What is the coach's philosophy of the game? How long has the coach been at the school, and how much longer does he plan to stay? How many players graduate on time? What kind of financial aid package is available, if not a scholarship?

Remember, however, that the questions themselves should come from the player. She should be the one asking them and evaluating the answers as they apply to her—not to her parents.

MAKING A VIDEOTAPE

A videotape can help a coach assess a player's abilities. Just be sure the camera angle is wide enough to show what the player does off the ball yet not so broad that the viewer misses specifics. The camera should be kept steady, facing the center of the field but with the entire field visible (slight elevation is ideal). Don't follow your son or daughter all over the field—shoot the game, not the player; then edit out the rest. Remember to announce at the beginning of the tape what number and color your child is wearing.

Some coaches prefer tapes of small-sided games—say, 4 v. 4 in a 40 x 30 field. This provides all the essentials of soccer—attacking, defending, supporting, decision making, positioning, technique, tactics, etc.—in a setting conducive to proper evaluation. The more competitive the game, the better the potential recruit's qualities will show. Finally, try to avoid sending copies; originals look best.

BEING A SECRETARY, NOT A BOSS

If a coach calls and your child is out, relay the message; do not engage the coach in a long conversation. Make sure your child receives coaches' mail; do not dictate replies. However, it is a good idea to check over your child's résumé for any egregious errors. A soccer résumé includes vital statistics (name, address, height, weight, position, date of graduation); team and individual accomplishments; and coaches' names and contact information. Of course, it should be scrupulously honest. It should also fill no more than one page; it needs to be succinct though complete. A schedule of upcoming games may be provided.

College soccer can benefit many young athletes. It enables them to meet interesting people, travel, and gain confidence. But college soccer is also a journey young athletes must take on their own. All a parent can do is help plan the trip, assist in packing, then wave good-bye and wish the soccer traveler well.

APPENDIX C
Finding Soccer News

MAGAZINES, NEWSPAPERS, AND NEWSLETTERS

Soccer America

The source for soccer news, this weekly publication covers every aspect of the game: youth, college, professional, domestic, international, men's, women's, you name it. A special camp issue appears each spring, and every four weeks the magazine presents a comprehensive listing of tournaments. Contact: Soccer America, P.O. Box 23704, Oakland, CA 94623; (510) 528-5000; *www.socceramerica.com*.

Soccer Jr.

This premier magazine for players ages eight to sixteen is published six times a year. Offered are features on players and soccer trends, how-to articles, questions and answers, lots of reader involvement, and frequent special issues. Contact: Soccer Jr., 27 Unquowa Rd., Fairfield, CT 06430; (203) 259-5766.

Soccer Now

The official publication of American Youth Soccer Organization (AYSO), this is mailed free to members. Contact: AYSO, 12501 S. Isis Ave., Hawthorne, CA 90250; 1-800-872-2976.

Regional Publications

Examples include *Soccer New* and *Southern Soccer Scene*. There are also numerous state association newspapers and newsletters.

WEB SITES

Each of these sites contains plenty of other links. Happy surfing!

American Youth Soccer Organization

www.ayso.org

FIFA, Soccer's International Governing Body

www.fifa.com

High School Soccer

www.kick.com

Soccer America Magazine

www.socceramerica.com

U.S. Soccer Federation,
the National Governing Body

www.us-soccer.com

U.S. Youth Soccer Association

www.usysa.org

APPENDIX D
Alphabet Soup

Confused about different levels of soccer? Wondering what the difference is between FIFA, ODP, and AYSO? You're not alone. The youth soccer world can be a strange place, awash in acronyms and drowning in a sea of initials other parents toss around like a helium-filled ball. Relax. You don't have to know too many buzz-words to sound like a parental pro; all you need are a few key ones. Here are the alphabet organizations that are most useful to know.

AYSO

This is the acronym for the American Youth Soccer Organization. For more than thirty years, this California-based group has run recreational-style soccer programs—both in conjunction with and (sometimes) as rivals to the national group, the U.S. Youth Soccer Association. AYSO registers over half a million young players each year. AYSO's motto is Everybody Plays.

FIFA

Pronounced "FEE-fuh," this is the French acronym for the international governing body of soccer. (Why is there no S for Soccer? Hint: *Football* is actually the French word for the game.) FIFA is based in Zurich. Every decision about soccer emanates from FIFA—although local leagues may modify certain rules to fit their needs.

MLS

Major League Soccer, founded in 1996, is the nation's top professional league. Below MLS is the minor-league USISL (United Systems of Independent Soccer Leagues), a hydra-headed organization consisting of the A-League (top rung), D-3 Pro League, W-League (for women), and PDSL (Premier Development Soccer League). The major indoor soccer league in the United States is the NPSL (National Professional Soccer League).

ODP

The Olympic Development Program provides the top youth players in the country an opportunity to receive extra training to advance up the soccer ladder to (hopefully) Olympic and World Cup teams. The program, administered by U.S. Youth Soccer, begins with state-level programs for top players. The state ODP programs feed into four regional ODP teams, out of which national youth teams are formed. ODP programs generally begin at the U-13 level.

SAY

The Soccer Association for Youth, based in Cincinnati, is the smallest of the three major youth soccer organizations in the United States. SAY teams are centered in the Midwest.

GLOSSARY

Corner kick: A restart taken by the opposite team after a ball has been kicked over the goal line by the defending team. The ball is kicked in from the corner of the field.

Defender: A defensive-minded player. Also called *fullback*.

Direct kick: A free kick awarded following a foul that involves physical contact, or a hand ball. A goal can be scored directly off the kick, without anyone else touching the ball.

Dribbling: Moving the ball, under control, with the feet.

Forward: An offensive-minded, front-line player.

Free kick: A restart taken by the opposite team after a foul. See *direct kick*, *indirect kick* and *penalty kick*.

Fullback: A defensive-minded player.

Goal area: The small box inside the larger penalty area, used to position the ball for a goal kick.

Goal kick: A restart taken by the opposite team after a ball has been kicked over the goal line by the attacking team. The ball is kicked out from the goal area.

Goal line: The out-of-bounds line at the end of each half. Also called *end line*.

Goalkeeper: The only player allowed to use hands (in the goal area only). Also called *goalie* or *keeper*.

Heading: Playing the ball with the head.

Indirect kick: A free kick awarded following a foul that does not involve physical contact or a hand ball. A goal cannot be scored directly off the kick; at least one other player (on either team) must touch the ball first.

Marking: Defending against a player.

Midfielder: A player expected to serve as a link between defenders and forwards.

Offside: A rule to prevent goal-hanging.

Penalty area: The area in which a goalkeeper may use hands; also the area in which a direct free kick is taken as a penalty kick. Also called *goal mouth*.

Penalty kick: A direct kick foul that occurs in the penalty area results in a penalty kick. The ball is placed twelve yards from goal, and the kicker has a free shot with only the goalkeeper guarding the goal.

Premier soccer: High-level, competitive youth soccer; also called, in various parts of the country, *classic*, *elite* and *travel* soccer.

Recreation soccer: Low-level, less-competitive youth soccer.

Red card: An ejection issued to a player or coach by the referee, for flagrant or continued misconduct.

Restart: Putting the ball back in play after it has gone out of bounds, or following a goal.

Short-sided soccer: Practice games or actual competition involving fewer than eleven players per team, utilizing a smaller field and smaller goals. Usually 3 v. 3, 4 v. 4, or 5 v. 5. Also called *small-sided soccer*.

Side line: The out-of-bounds line running along the side of the field.

Stopper: A central defender whose primary job is to "stop" the most dangerous forward.

Striker: An offensive-minded, front-line player. Also called *forward*.

Sweeper: A defender whose primary job is to move laterally and "sweep" away any balls that get through.

Tackling: Attempting to win the ball away from another player using the legs.

Training session: Practice session.

Throw-in: The method by which play is restarted after the ball goes over the sideline.

Wall pass: A pass from one player to another that is immediately returned to the first player, as if off a wall. Also called *give-and-go* or *one-two*.

Wing: The outside of the field. Also called *flank*.

Yellow card: A warning (or caution) issued to a player or coach by the referee.

INDEX